Miniature Magic

150 PATCHWORK PATTERNS

Gay Imbach

with

Joyce Jesperson Bacon

Acknowledgements:

We wish to acknowledge the special help of Dee Hall, who unhesitatingly met every deadline and provided us with the delightful sketches found throughout the book: Naomi and Frank Taylor, Marty Sandell, Mildred Morgon and Helen Imbach, who have shared their talents and knowledge with us, and have offered unending encouragement, inspiration and support in the preparation of this book.

Our heartful thanks to Joan Aasen, Wanda Belcher, Nancy Brosious, Nancy Downs, Helen Imbach, Sharon Joor, Shannon Newton and Joan Womack, who so graciously permitted us to photograph their creations.

And most of all, we thank our husbands, Chris and Nelson, and our families for their undying patience, support and encouragement, and without whom this book would not have been.

Front Cover: Mexican Star Quilt by Wanda Belcher. 4" Blocks.
Star-Within-A-Star, Sampler Quilt and Tote Bag
Patchwork by Gay Imbach. 6" and 4" Blocks.

Back Cover: Decorator Items and Doll Quilt by Gay Imbach.
6" Blocks.

Published by: imbach Publications
246 Greengates, Corona, CA 91720

Copyright© 1981 by Gay Imbach and
Joyce Jesperson Bacon

Second Edition 1982

Library of Congress Catalog Card Number 81-90682

ISBN 0-9607648-0-1

Manufactured in the United States of America.

Illustrations by Dee Hall

Dedication

We dedicate this book to our students and quilting friends who have enriched our lives and shared in the quilting experience, and to our grandmother and mother, Clarissa Jesperson, who inspired the love of sewing in our lives.

FOREWARD

Handmade quilts have been a part of our lives through the years, but it was not until about nine years ago that the interest was re-kindled and eventually set aflame to the stage of a consuming and challenging craft. As we shared our creations with others and displayed our quilts at shows and fairs, we received repeated requests to teach others, and thus in the early 70's began a new and rewarding experience in our lives.

By this time our beds were covered, the closets were filled, almost every new mother had received a quilt as a shower gift, and we had boxes of unquilted tops in the attic. There were so many patterns we wanted to try, sketch pads full of ideas waiting to 'materialize,' and the new dimension of teaching was adding boxes full of sample blocks within already bulging walls. The full-sized quilt on the big frame in the parlor had hardly been touched in two years (except to rearrange the dust cover and dislodge a retiring cat) and something had to change.

We found that most of our students were career women, busy housewives, and mothers of active growing children with limited time for self and hobbies. Their interest in patchwork and quilting was spawned by the multitude of pictures and publicity afforded quilting by the bi-centennial, but time and facility decidedly affected their motiviation to participate in the craft if it meant making a full sized quilt. It was a task many undertook but few completed. As a result of our student's needs, as well as our own dilemma, we were prompted to miniaturize our efforts without decreasing our interest, the challenge to create, and the satisfaction of making completed projects.

The reaction to 'miniaturized' patchwork was inspiring. The busy young wife and mother, the career woman, and the traditional quilter alike loudly acclaimed the new horizons available through the small scale patchwork. Since there were no miniature patchwork pattern books available, a great deal of our time was spent custom drafting patterns for our students as well as for our personal use.

It was these experiences that prompted us to undertake this endeavor. It is our sincere hope that this book will serve to provide the novice patchworker and quilter with an introduction to basic patchwork construction and quilting techniques, provide a resource for all quilters for miniature patterns, and provide a springboard of ideas and inspirations for unique and individualized projects beyond the scope of traditional patchwork.

Contents

INTRODUCTION

Welcome to the world of miniature patchwork! For the experienced quilter and the novice alike we hope this book will help you project magic into your creations by providing an alternative or addition to the more common large scale patchwork blocks.

Working with miniature patchwork is easy, fun, challenging and rewarding. The satisfaction of creating and exploring with fabric, patterns and color is enhanced, and the applications are unlimited. For the modern day working woman, restricted by time and responsibilities in the present day world, working with miniatures opens the door for increased pleasure in the field of patchwork and quilting. No longer overwhelmed or discouraged by the prospect of making a full-sized quilt, limited by lack of facility and time to put it in a large frame and quilt it, she now can experience the same satisfaction and challenge enjoyed by the full-time homemaker quilter. For the traditional quilter, miniature patchwork affords the opportunity to individualize and customize familiar patterns with added interest and intrigue.

This is primarily a pattern book. Although basic instructions in patchwork block construction and quilting are included, no attempt has been made to provide explicit and comprehensive instruction in the 'how to' phase of quiltmaking. There are many excellent basic instruction books available in stores today, a few of which are included in the bibliography. We have addressed the need for miniature patchwork borders by including a variety of designs, some of which are presented in more than one size. The original and traditional quilting designs have been scaled to compliment miniature patchwork projects.

In selecting the patterns for inclusion in this collection, we have tried to meet the needs of the novice piecer and experienced quiltmaker alike. For those not yet accustomed to working with small scale patchwork, we recommend beginning with blocks consisting of a minimal number of squares and right triangles before attempting more challenging constructions. Included in the pattern collection are several original block designs, specified by an asterisk in the pattern index. Some patterns are presented in more than one size to facilitate easy construction of 'paired' or matching creations, and to increase design possibilities. A minimal number of larger conventional-sized patterns have been included by special request of quilters who have found delight in using them in conjunction with their miniature patchwork. The patterns selected in this category are original designs, with one exception, and therefore are not available in existing pattern publications.

Whatever your interest, whether it is to enhance a full-sized quilt, provide another dimension in interior decorating, customize a wardrobe, reclothe that treasured doll from your childhood, create charming and personal gifts of love for favored friends or loved ones, we hope this book brings you pleasure, increases your interest and facination with patchwork, and helps you to personalize your heirlooms for present as well as future enjoyment.

Endless design possibilities exist in the drafting and construction of patchwork blocks. We believe that the designs created by us and so designated are indeed original. We recognize, however, that the possibility exists that like or common designs may have existed at some previous time or place unknown to us. If this be the case, there has been no intention on our part to unjustly claim credit for someone else's design, and it has been done in innocence.

Fundamentals of Patchwork and Quilting

SUPPLIES

Most of the supplies needed for patchwork are common household items you probably already have on hand.

A ruler, tracing paper, lightweight cardboard, and paper-cutting scissors will be used to make the patterns. Medium-fine sandpaper placed rough side up under fabric will prevent it from shifting while pattern pieces are being traced.

Graph paper and colored pencils are extremely useful for pre-planning a project. By using the pencils to shade in a design sketch you will be able to pre-determine the effect that will be achieved by the colors designated for the finished product. Graph paper with 1/4" or 1/8" grid is also convenient for determining and marking seam allowances for pattern pieces.

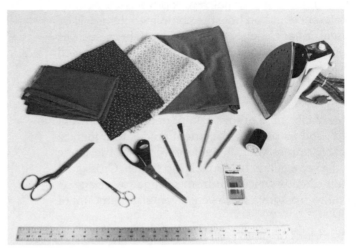

A #2 lead pencil, a dressmaker's chalk or a water erasable pen may be used to draw a pattern or quilting designs on fabric.

General sewing supplies include a pair of sharp dressmaker's shears, embroidery scissors, needles ("Sharps" for general sewing, "Betweens" for quilting), sharp pins (glass-headed pins are easiest to work with), a pin cushion, a good fitting thimble, iron and an ironing board. If you are planning on quilting your patchwork you will need both general sewing thread and quilting thread. Extra strong thread is made especially for quilting and comes in a wide variety of colors.

Cotton and polyester batting for quilted projects is readily available in stores today, and comes cello packaged and cut in pre-determined standard quilt sizes. Polyester batting may also be purchased by the yard, and many merchants offer a choice of thicknesses. The heavier batts are generally used for comforters, while the medium to thin weights are used for quilts, clothing, boutiques and other small items.

A portable quilting frame, to hold you miniature patchwork project taut for hand quilting, may easily be constructed at home with minimal expense.

Definitions

Backing: The bottom or lining layer of a quilt.

Batting: The filler used between the top and backing of a quilt. (Commercial battings are available in cotton and in various thicknesses of polyester).

Binding: The piece of fabric used to cover the outside raw edges of a quilt.

Block: One section of patchwork containing a complete design, used alone, repeated, or combined with others for an overall design.

Borders: Strips of a single fabric or combinations of fabrics pieced together to form a design and used to frame units within a quilt or the quilt itself.

Coverlet: A small bed covering consisting of a top and backing, usually unquilted.

Lattice: Strips of fabric used to frame or separate individual blocks within a quilt.

Marking: The method used to draw pattern pieces or quilting designs on fabric.

Piece: The joining of pieces to larger units.

Patchwork: A fabric unit consisting of small pieces of fabric sewn together to form a larger unit.

Quilt: A unit consisting of 3 layers, a top, filler and a backing.

Quilting: The joining of the 3 layers of a quilt with tiny running stitches.

Putting in: The process of putting the three layers of a quilt into a quilting frame to hold even tautness while the quilting is done.

Template: One piece of a pattern, usually made of cardboard, plastic, metal or sandpaper, used in transferring a shape to fabric.

Fabrics

The fabrics you choose for your patchwork projects will depend on personal preference and on how the completed items will be used. As a general rule, closely woven opaque fabrics such as 100% cotton, muslin and cotton/polyester blends are well suited for both patchwork and quilting. Check to be sure that they are color-fast and that they have been pre-shrunk. If in doubt, it is generally a good idea to wash and iron them before using.

The grain lines of fabric are of special importance in patchwork sewing, and are used as pattern placement guides to minimize fabric distortion. As a reminder, the straight grain of the fabric runs parallel to the selvage and has virtually no stretch. Crossgrain refers to the weft threads which run from selvage to selvage. A slight pulling on the crossgrain will reveal a very slight amount of stretch. (Fig. 1)

The greatest amount of stretch will be found on the diagonal or bias. To determine the true bias, fold the fabric so that the crossgrain edge runs parallel to a selvage forming a 45 degree triangle. (Fig 2) The folded edge has considerable stretch and readily distorts with pulling or tugging.

To minimize fabric distortion, always try to place pattern templates so that the maximum number of sides are parallel to the straight and crossgrains of the fabric.

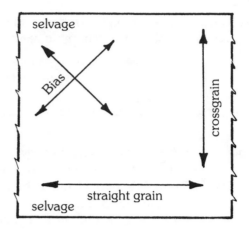

Figure 1. Grain lines of fabric.

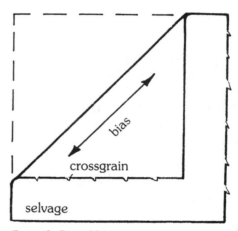

Figure 2. Bias of fabric.

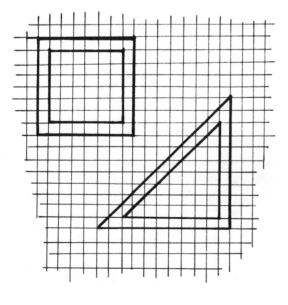

Figure 3. Adding seam allowance to templates.

Templates

Templates are the pattern pieces for each shape in a patchwork pattern. The patterns in this book are actual size and seam allowances must be added. Many quilters prefer a 1/8 inch seam allowance for the 3 inch patchwork and graduate to a 1/4 inch seam allowance for the larger patterns.

For hand piecing, templates are cut the exact size of each pattern piece and the seam allowance is added during the fabric cutting. To make the templates, accurately trace the pattern and then transfer the tracings to cardboard or plastic. It is usually a good idea to number the templates for easy identification.

When doing machine piecing the seam allowance is included in the template. A relatively simple and accurate way of adding the seam is to trace the pattern pieces onto 1/4" or 1/8" translucent graph paper, add the seam allowance with the aid of the grid markings (Fig. 3), then transfer the enlarged tracings onto the cardboard. Again, number the individual templates for easy identification when working with them.

The need for accuracy cannot be over-emphasized. Small inaccuracies in templates can magnify into unbelievable frustrations in making the finshed product.

Marking Fabric

A fine point pencil or marking device is recommended for tracing the pattern templates on fabric. Lay your fabric, wrong side up, on a smooth flat surface. Slip a piece of sandpaper, rough side up, under the fabric to prevent it from moving during marking. For hand piecing, templates should be placed approximately ½ inch apart to allow for the addition of seam allowances when cutting the patches. (Fig. 4) Take care to trace the templates accurately, the marked lines will be the actual sewing lines.

For machine patchwork, the templates may be placed adjacent to one another with a common cutting line if the pattern shapes are the same or compatable. Since the seam allowance is included in the template, the marked line is the cutting line.

Analyzing Patchwork Patterns

Before beginning the actual construction of your miniature block, study the block sketch and visually break the pattern down into natural geometric groupings. For example, the Windmill pattern (Fig. 5a) contains 4 identical squares consisting of three triangles each. These squares can be further dissected into two triangles consisting of 1 large and 2 smaller triangles. Construction would begin with the smallest units, i.e. all four pairs of the small triangles would be joined first, then joined to the larger triangles of equal size. The resulting squares would be joined in pairs, and the block would be completed with the stitching of the center seam.

The basic principle you should keep in mind is that the sequence of construction you choose should allow for as much straight seam piecing as possible. Use this method of visually dissecting all your patchwork blocks to find the way it may be pieced before you begin sewing. Visually dissect the blocks in Fig. 5b and 5c.

Dissection of Patchwork blocks.

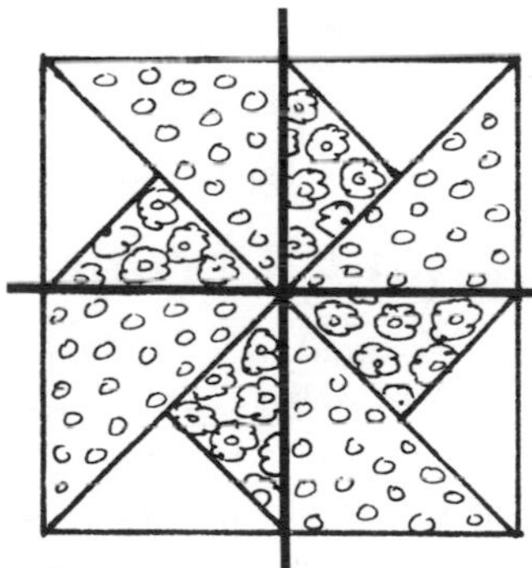

Figure 5a.

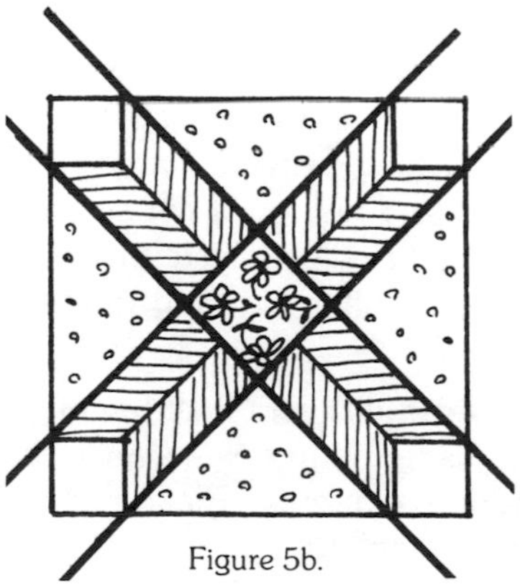

Figure 5b.

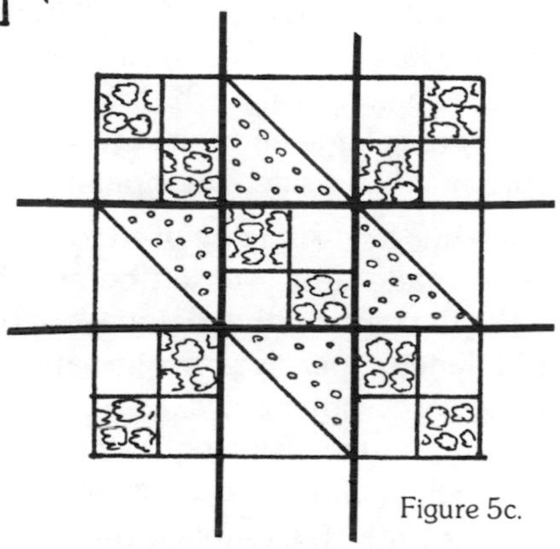

Figure 5c.

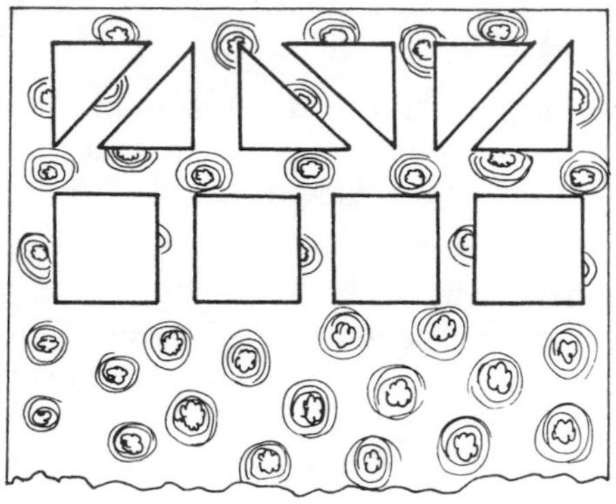

Figure 4.
Template
Placement
on fabric.

Patchwork Piecing

Patchwork blocks may be assembled by hand piecing or by machine sewing. Knowing and understanding the principles of both methods will help you decide which is right for you, and help you in assembling a variety of challenging patterns.

For hand piecing you will need sharp sewing needles and standard weight sewing thread. Lay your patchwork pieces right sides together, carefully matching the stitching lines, and pin securely. Begin sewing at the end of the seam line, taking a series of small running stitches on the needle at one time. Take a securing backstitch every time the needle is reinserted into the fabric. Secure the thread at the end of the seam line with two or three back stitches or a small knot. Hand pieced blocks are not pressed until the entire block has been completed.

As you recall, templates for machine piecing include seam allowances, therefore the block pieces will not have stitching lines on them. A ¼ inch seam allowance can be measured on most sewing machines by aligning the edge of the fabric with the edge of the presser foot. If the pressure foot on your machine is not ¼ inch wide, or if your are using a narrower seam allowance, place a piece of colored tape on the sewing machine base plate the desired distance from the needle and parallel to the pressure foot. Use the tape as a guide when feeding the patches thru the machine. Feed the pieces thru the sewing machine in a continuous line. (Fig. 6) As you reach the end of the first unit lay the next one down and continue the stitching, leaving only a short distance of thread between pieces. After all of the units have been stitched, clip them apart. A great deal of time can be saved with this continuous sewing technique.

Press the seams after the units have been stitched and before joining them to other units. Seams should be pressed to one side, preferably to the side of the darkest material so that they will not show thru to the front of the fabric. (Fig. 7)

Figure 6. Continuous Sewing in patchwork piecing.

Figure 7. Press seams to one side.

Quilting Designs

Quilting refers to the stitching that is done to hold the top, batting and back securely together. It adds beauty and accents and defines a pattern or design. Personal preference determines where and how much quilting is done.

Traditional quilting refers to the elaborate quilting designs of our ancestors. Enhanced by spectacular feather wreaths, flowing cables and scrolls, and row after row of delicate stitches ¼ inch to ½ inch apart, the quilts of yesteryear have become treasured heirlooms. Carded cotton and wool were commonly used for the filler and close stitching was necessary to stabilize the batting and prevent it from shifting during use. Although the polyester batting used today does not require the same over-all stitching, traditional designs are still being used to enhance and beautify quilts, patchwork clothing and boutiques.

Outline quilting is frequently used by the modern quilter. The quilting stitches follow the lines of individual pieces of the patchwork blocks, and are commonly placed 1/8 to 1/4 inch from the seam line. They tend to intensify the patchwork design by giving it a dimensional look, and optical illusions can be created by accenting selected shapes or colors within a pattern. (Fig. 8)

Figure 8. Contemporary and Traditional quilting combined to enhance the patchwork.

Marking for Quilting

If your miniature patchwork project is to be quilted, the designs may be marked on the fabric with a medium soft lead pencil (a No. 2 works fine), an artist's white chalk pencil, or with a tracing wheel and dressmaker's carbon.

Figure 12. Completed wall hanging ready for hanging.

Assembly of Quilts and Wall Hangings

The assembly sequence will depend on the process that will be used to finish your project. If the miniature patchwork has been incorporated into a full sized quilt it will be assembled as a 'textile sandwich,' consisting of the backing material, batting and pieced top. Lay the backing right side down on a flat surface, cover with the batting and the top, right side up. Baste the three layers together to prevent them from shifting during quilting. (Fig. 9)

The outside edges of miniaturized quilts and wall hangings may be finished before the quilting is done. In this instance the layers will be assembled in a different sequence. Place the top and backing on a flat surface, right sides together, and cover with the batting. (Fig. 10) Pin and stitch around all sides, leaving an opening large enough to turn the item right side out. (Fig. 11) Turn and blind stitch the opening closed.

If fabric tabs are to be used to hang your project they will need to be made and inserted before the top edge is stitched. To make the tabs cut the material double the desired finished width and length, plus seam allowance. Fold the material in half lengthwise with right sides together and stitch the long side forming a tube. Turn right side out, fold in half with raw edges together, and insert the tabs between the top and backing fabrics of your project. Complete the stitching and turn right side out. Blind stitch the opening and quilt if desired. (Fig. 12)

Figure 9. The 'textile sandwich.'

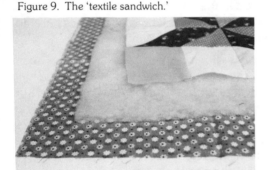

Figure 10. The batting, top and backing assembled for stitching.

Figure 11. Leave an opening in one side to turn the quilt right side out.

Patchwork in Clothing

One of the most popular uses of miniature patchwork is in the embellishment of clothing. Skirts, jackets, shirts, aprons, tunics, dresses and slacks are the most popular items selected for patchwork accents. Miniature borders or patchwork blocks used individually, in repeats or in combinations, add an intriguing new dimension to a wardrobe. The patchwork may be appliqued onto existing clothing or incorporated into garments during their initial construction.

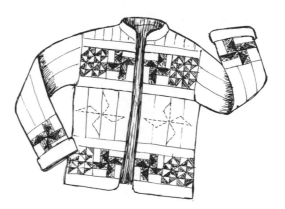

Commercial patterns with basic straight-line styling lend themselves well to the incorporation of patchwork detailing. Begin by determining the exact area into which the patchwork will be added. Mark the pattern piece involved with splice lines to dissect the pattern as shown in Figure 13. Cut the pattern on the splice lines and add seam allowances to all cut edges. Using the dissected pattern pieces, cut the required fabrics and patchwork section. Re-assemble the units to create the original configuration of the total pattern piece. Complete the garment according to pattern directions. The patchwork area may be lined to conceal the multiple seams. Quilting is optional.

Figure 13. Dissect the pattern for insertion of the patchwork section.

Quilting

Quilting adds depth and dimension to patchwork and enhances the overall design of patchwork projects. Extra strong needles and thread are used for quilting. Called 'Between,' the needles can be purchased in individual sizes or in assortment packages with sizes ranging from a No. 5 thru No. 10 needles. We recommend beginning with a No. 7 or No. 8 needle. Quilting thread is specifically labeled for that purpose and can be purchased in a wide variety of colors.

Begin by cutting a section of thread approximately 18 inches in length, and make a loop knot on one end. Using a single thread, insert the needle into the surface fabric a needle distance away from the quilting line and re-surface the needle where you will begin quilting. Gently tug on the thread until the knot pops thru the fabric and lodges in the batting. Using a thimble on the middle finger of your right hand, guide the needle through the fabric, taking three or four small stitches at one time. Use a finger of the left hand under the quilt to guide and assist the needle, making sure that the stitches go thru all three layers. To end a line of quilting, take one or two small back stitches, or make a loop knot in the thread and conceal it in the layer of batting as before.

Frame Quilting

A quilting frame is used to keep the quilt taut and to prevent the 3 layers from shifting during quilting. (Fig. 14) We recommend a 'quilt-on-the-go' frame, consisting of four ¼" × 2" × 24" slats with strips of fabric secured to the inside edges of them for pinning to the item that will be quilted. In addition to the obvious advantage of being portable because it is small, this type of frame adapts freely to the irregular configurations required for boutique quilting, is expandable, and allows four-way tension control. In addition to the standard 24" commercial frame, we have a second frame with 12" bars which we use singly and in combination with the larger frame to achieve an even wider range of shapes and sizes.

Figure 14. A quilt frame holds the fabric taut for quilting.

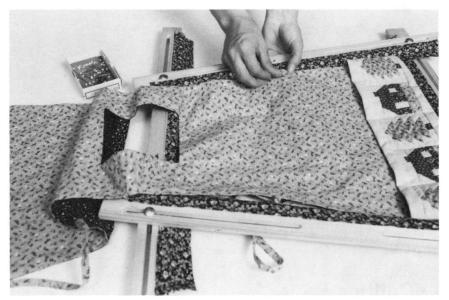

Figure 15. A small project is placed on top of the frame and pinned to the fabric strips.

When using the frame for small items, adjust the size of the frame so that the fabric strips overlap the outside edges of the project to be quilted by about ½." Lay the project on top of the frame and pin the strips to the project as shown in Fig. 15. Do not tighten the securing bolts on the frame or put any tension on the project until after all four sides have been pinned. Conceal the points of the pins in the fabric to keep them out of the way when the quilting is being accomplished. Tighten the frame bolts and adjust the tension on the project so that the material is taut. If seams within the project are pulled or distorted the tension is too tight. Obvious sags or wrinkles indicate that the tension needs to to be increased.

When the project to be quilted is larger than the frame place the frame on top of the project to facilitate pinning. (Fig. 16) Extend the frame to within approximately one inch of it's maximum expansion range to allow adequate space for adjusting the tension after the pinning has been completed. Pin the fabric strips on the frame to the project as before, and adjust tension on the project when the frame bolts are tightened after pinning.

Figure 16. The frame is placed on the top of larger projects to facilitate pinning to the fabric strips.

Many of the miniaturized quilts, wall hangings and similar projects are completed as described in the section on assembly before they are quilted. The frame is placed in the center of the project and as the quilting progresses it is moved outward. Basting is optional. (Fig. 17)

Figure 17. The pre-finished miniature quilt is ready for quilting.

Figure 18. Full-sized miniaturized quilts may also be quilted on the portable frame.

Full-sized miniaturized quilts may also be quilted on the portable frame. (Fig. 18) The frame is used in the same manner as the traditional oval hoop, but it provides increased control over tension and permits quilting all the way to the outside edges of the quilt. (Fig. 19) The large quilts are basted and the quilting begins in the center of the quilt and progresses outward to the edges. While the frame is being pinned in position, the left hand is placed under the quilt to assist in the pinning process.

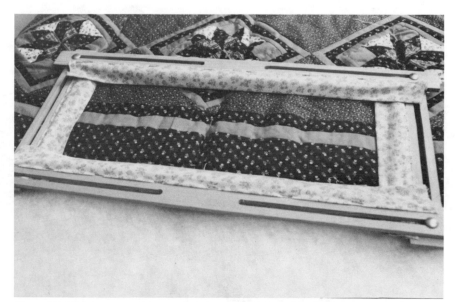

Figure 19. The frame may be moved to the outside edge of the quilt.

Patchwork Patterns

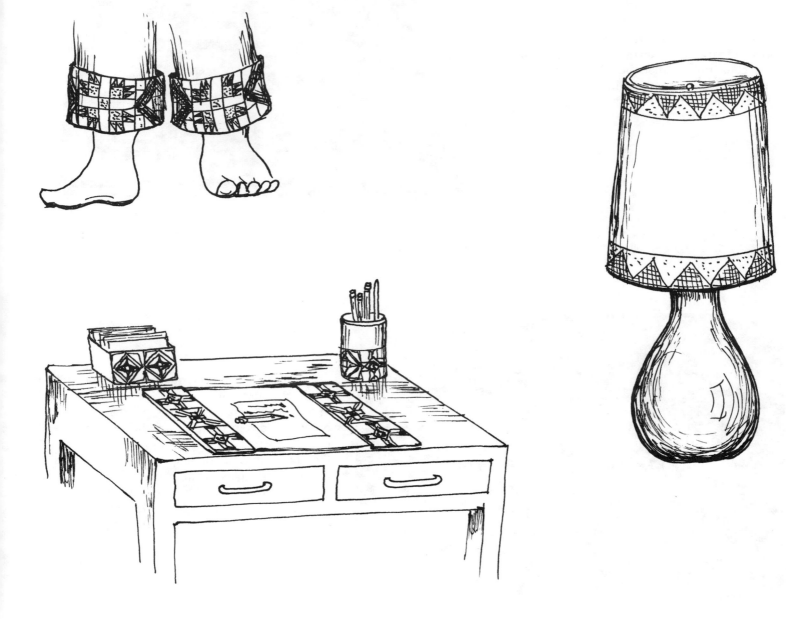

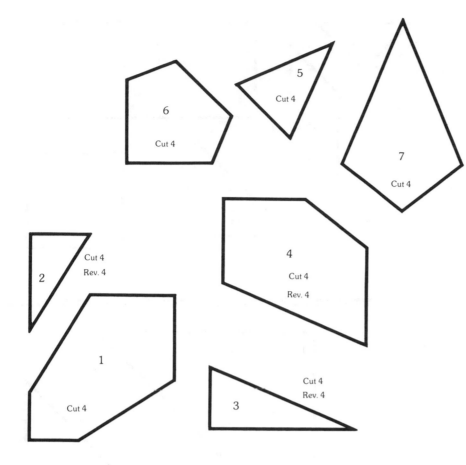

6
Cut 4

5
Cut 4

7
Cut 4

2
Cut 4
Rev. 4

4
Cut 4
Rev. 4

1
Cut 4

3
Cut 4
Rev. 4

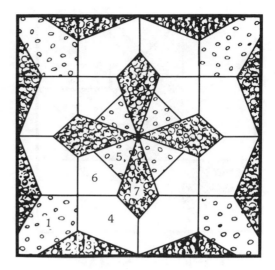

*SUNSHINE
6" BLOCK

4
Cut 8

1
Cut 4

2
Cut 4
Rev. 4

3
Cut 4
Rev. 4

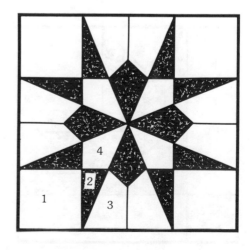

ST. LOUIS STAR
6" BLOCK

Add Seam Allowance

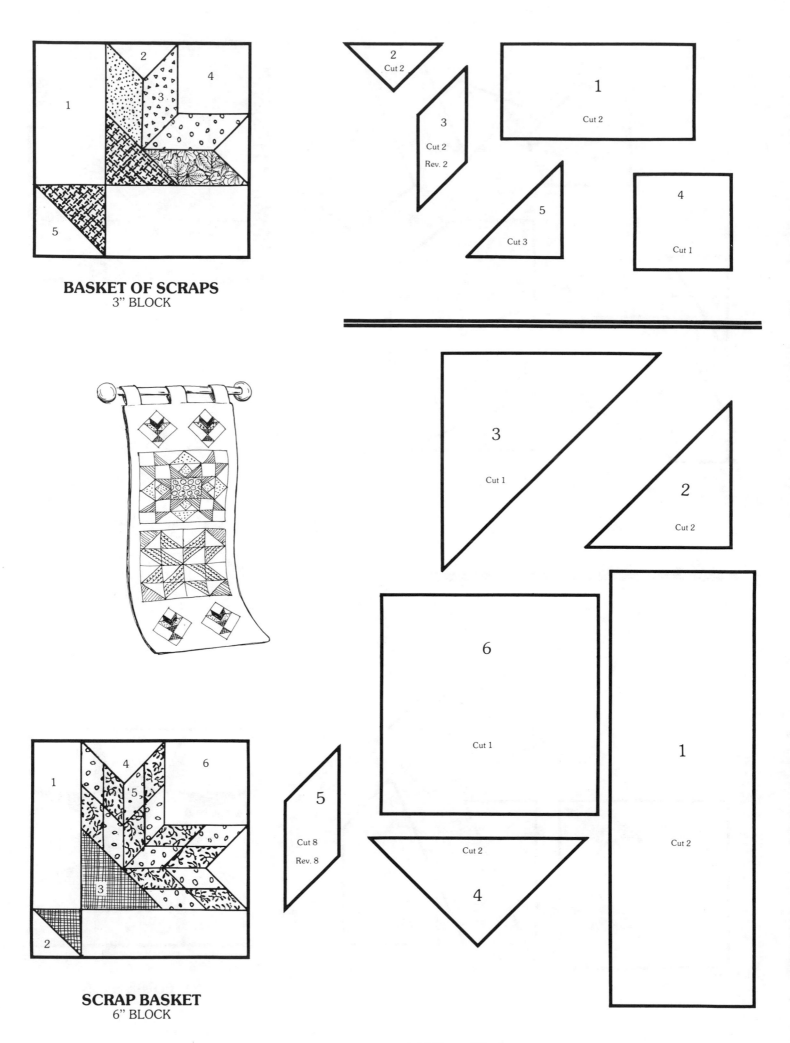

BASKET OF SCRAPS
3" BLOCK

2
Cut 2

3
Cut 2
Rev. 2

1
Cut 2

5
Cut 3

4
Cut 1

3
Cut 1

2
Cut 2

6
Cut 1

5
Cut 8
Rev. 8

1
Cut 2

4
Cut 2

SCRAP BASKET
6" BLOCK

Add Seam Allowance

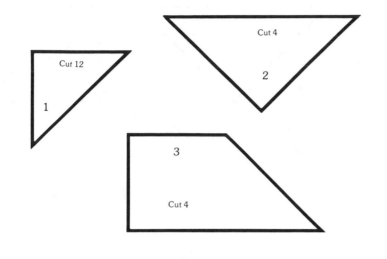

Cut 12

1

Cut 4

2

3

Cut 4

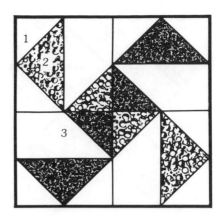

NEXT DOOR NEIGHBOR
4" BLOCK

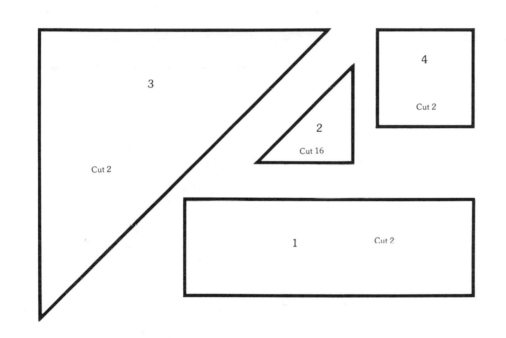

3

Cut 2

2

Cut 16

4

Cut 2

1   Cut 2

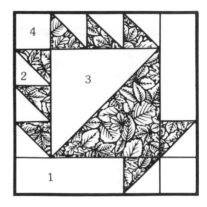

CAKE STAND
5" BLOCK

3

Cut 1

2

Cut 12

1

Cut 16

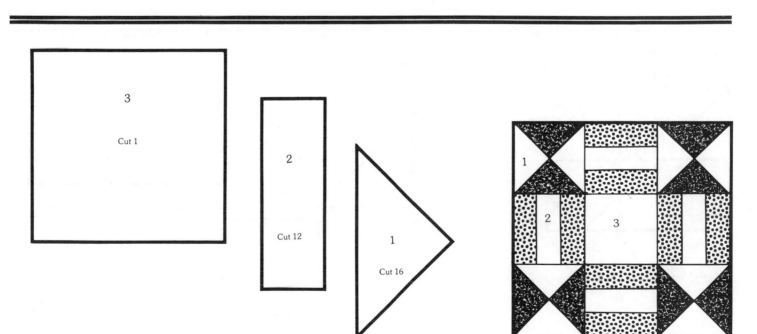

LONDON ROADS
6" BLOCK

Add Seam Allowance

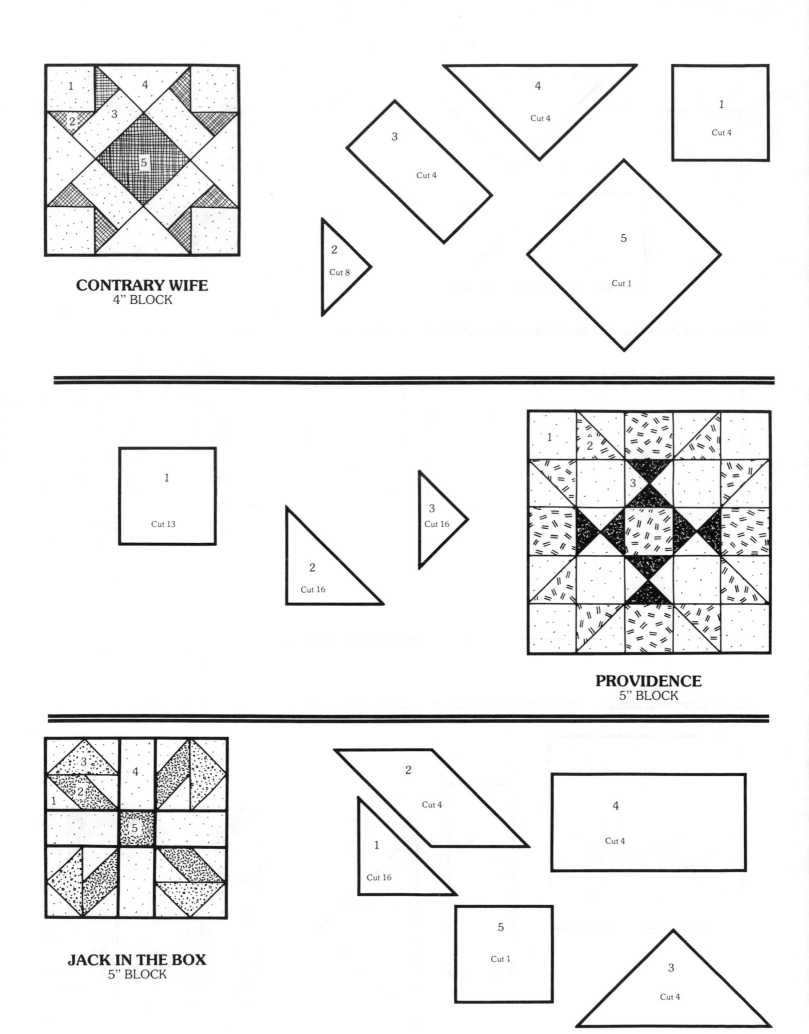

CONTRARY WIFE
4" BLOCK

3 Cut 4

4 Cut 4

2 Cut 8

1 Cut 4

5 Cut 1

1 Cut 13

2 Cut 16

3 Cut 16

PROVIDENCE
5" BLOCK

JACK IN THE BOX
5" BLOCK

2 Cut 4

1 Cut 16

4 Cut 4

5 Cut 1

3 Cut 4

Add Seam Allowance

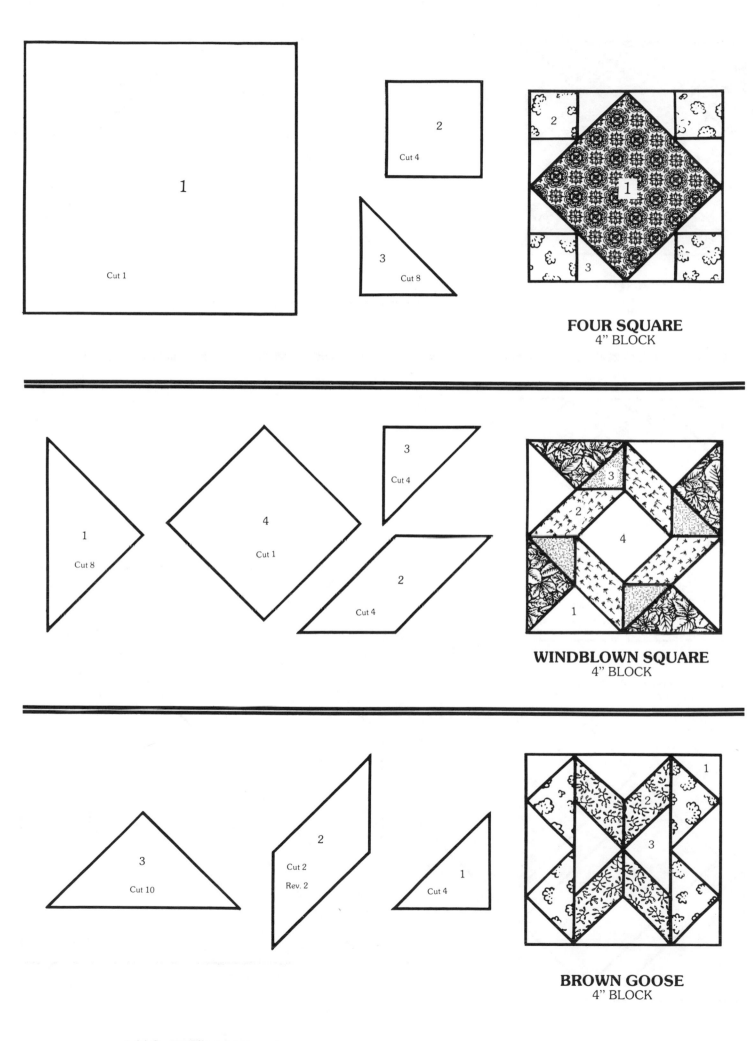

1

Cut 1

2

Cut 4

3

Cut 8

1

FOUR SQUARE
4" BLOCK

1

Cut 8

4

Cut 1

3

Cut 4

2

Cut 4

3

2

4

1

WINDBLOWN SQUARE
4" BLOCK

3

Cut 10

2

Cut 2

Rev. 2

1

Cut 4

1

2

3

BROWN GOOSE
4" BLOCK

Add Seam Allowance

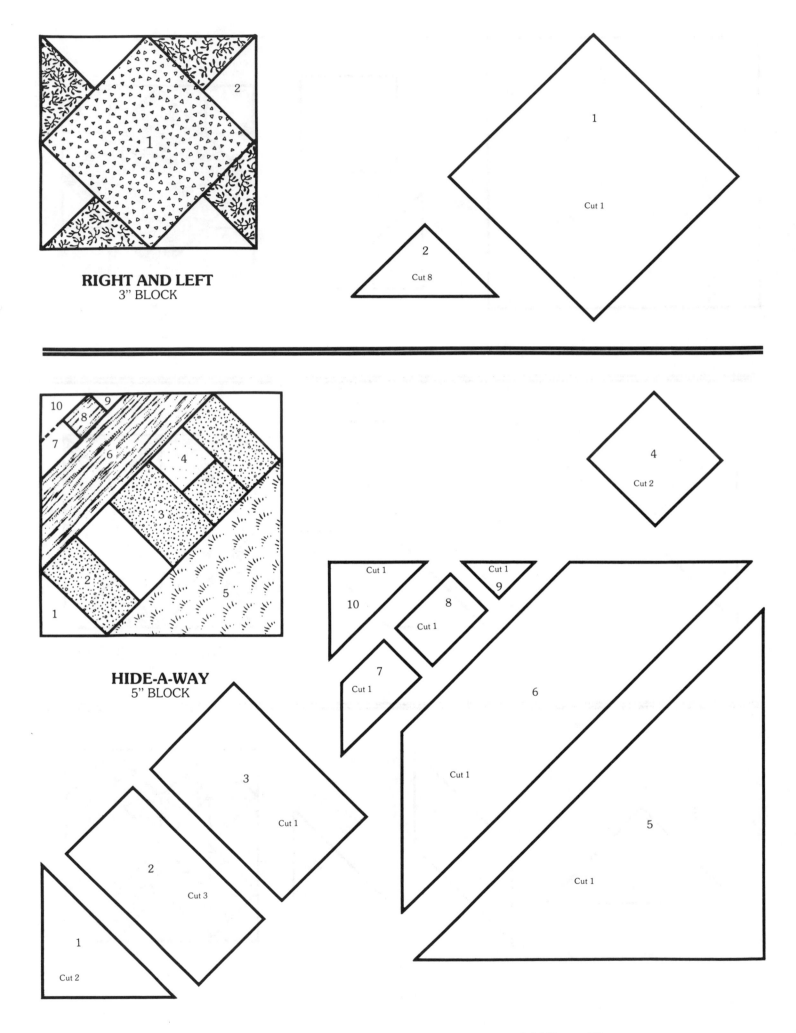

RIGHT AND LEFT
3" BLOCK

1
Cut 1

2
Cut 8

HIDE-A-WAY
5" BLOCK

4
Cut 2

10
Cut 1

8
Cut 1

9
Cut 1

7
Cut 1

6
Cut 1

5
Cut 1

3
Cut 1

2
Cut 3

1
Cut 2

Add Seam Allowance

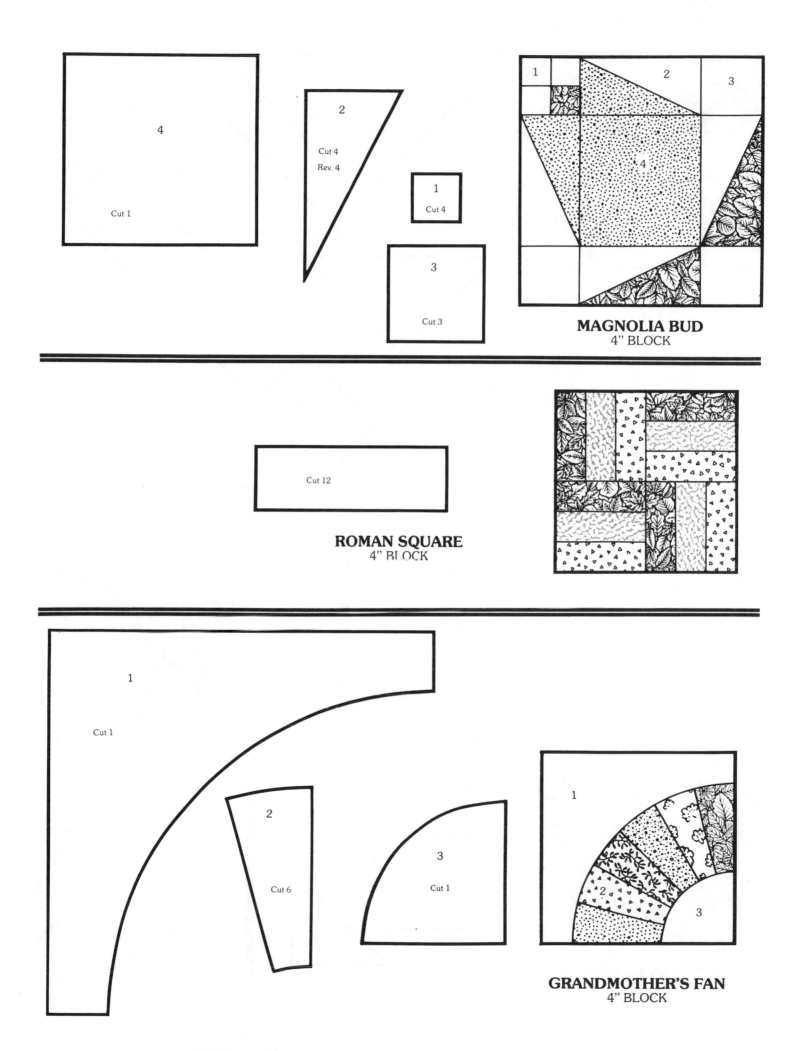

4

Cut 1

2

Cut 4
Rev. 4

1

Cut 4

3

Cut 3

1 2 3

4

MAGNOLIA BUD
4" BLOCK

Cut 12

ROMAN SQUARE
4" BLOCK

1

Cut 1

2

Cut 6

3

Cut 1

1

2

3

GRANDMOTHER'S FAN
4" BLOCK

Add Seam Allowance

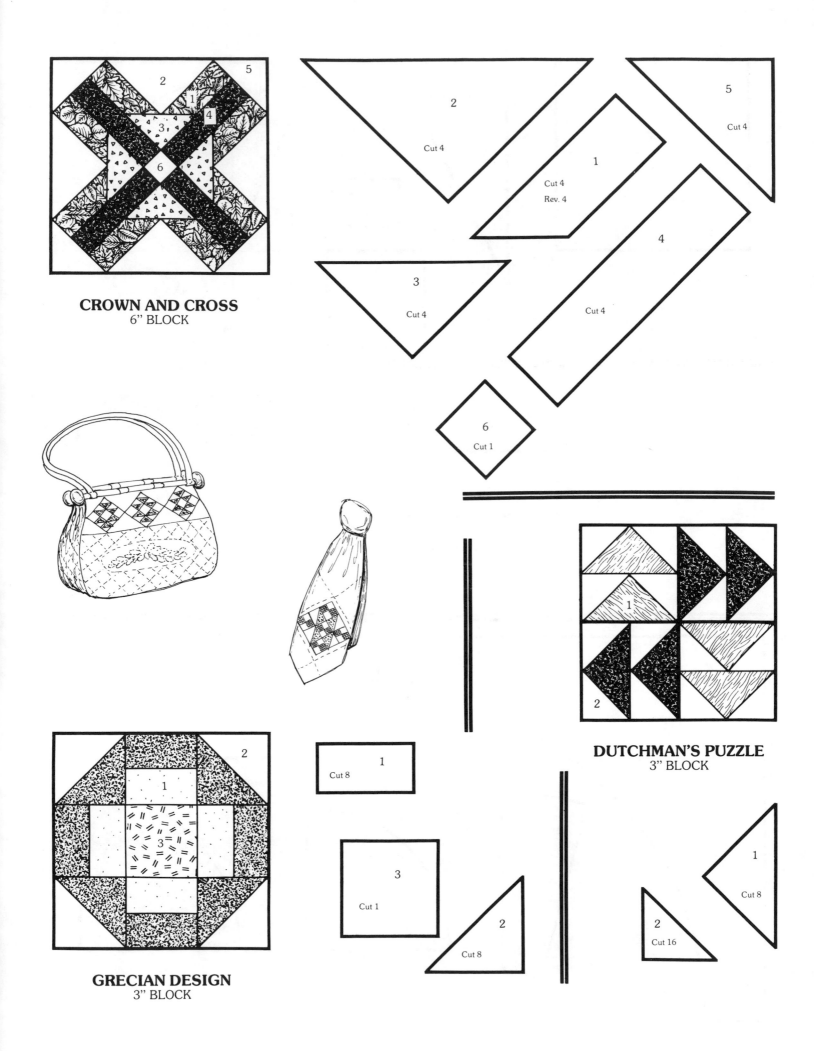

CROWN AND CROSS
6" BLOCK

2

Cut 4

1
Cut 4
Rev. 4

5
Cut 4

4
Cut 4

3
Cut 4

6
Cut 1

DUTCHMAN'S PUZZLE
3" BLOCK

1
Cut 8

3
Cut 1

2
Cut 8

1
Cut 8

2
Cut 16

GRECIAN DESIGN
3" BLOCK

Add Seam Allowance

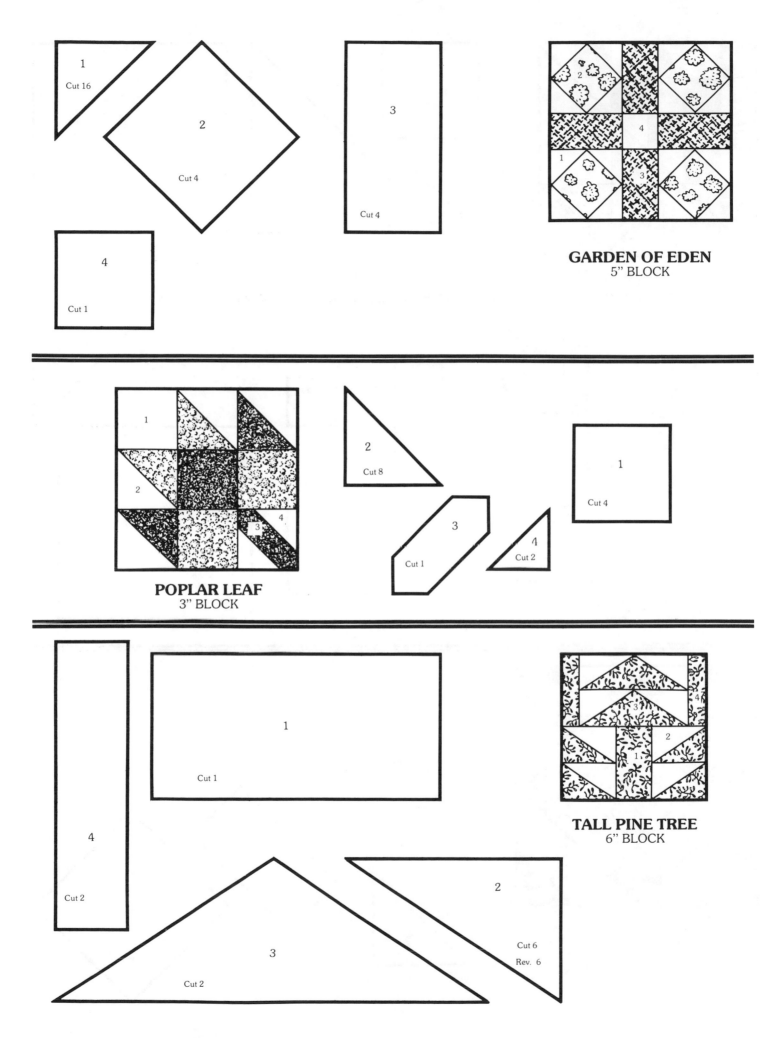

1
Cut 16

2
Cut 4

3
Cut 4

4
Cut 1

GARDEN OF EDEN
5" BLOCK

POPLAR LEAF
3" BLOCK

2
Cut 8

3
Cut 1

4
Cut 2

1
Cut 4

TALL PINE TREE
6" BLOCK

1
Cut 1

4
Cut 2

3
Cut 2

2
Cut 6
Rev. 6

Add Seam Allowance

23

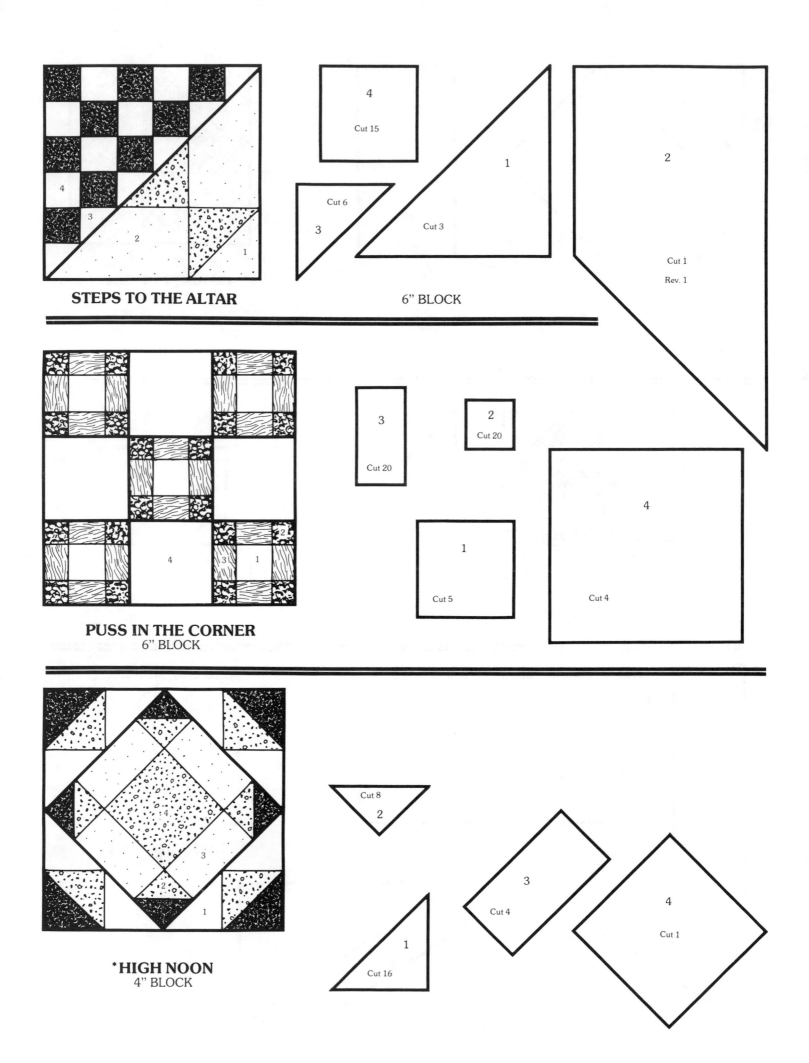

STEPS TO THE ALTAR

4

Cut 15

Cut 6

3

1

Cut 3

2

Cut 1

Rev. 1

6" BLOCK

PUSS IN THE CORNER
6" BLOCK

3

Cut 20

2

Cut 20

1

Cut 5

4

Cut 4

*HIGH NOON
4" BLOCK

Cut 8

2

3

Cut 4

4

Cut 1

1

Cut 16

Add Seam Allowance

1

Cut 4

6

Cut 4

4

Cut 8

2

Cut 16

3

Cut 8

5

Cut 1

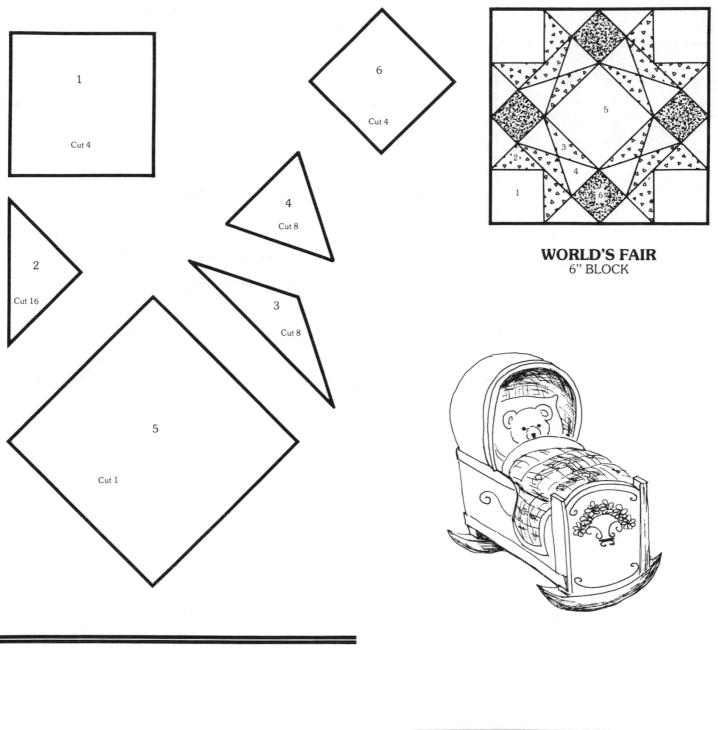

WORLD'S FAIR
6" BLOCK

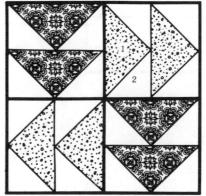

1

Cut 8

2

Cut 16

Add Seam Allowance

DUTCHMAN'S PUZZLE
4" BLOCK

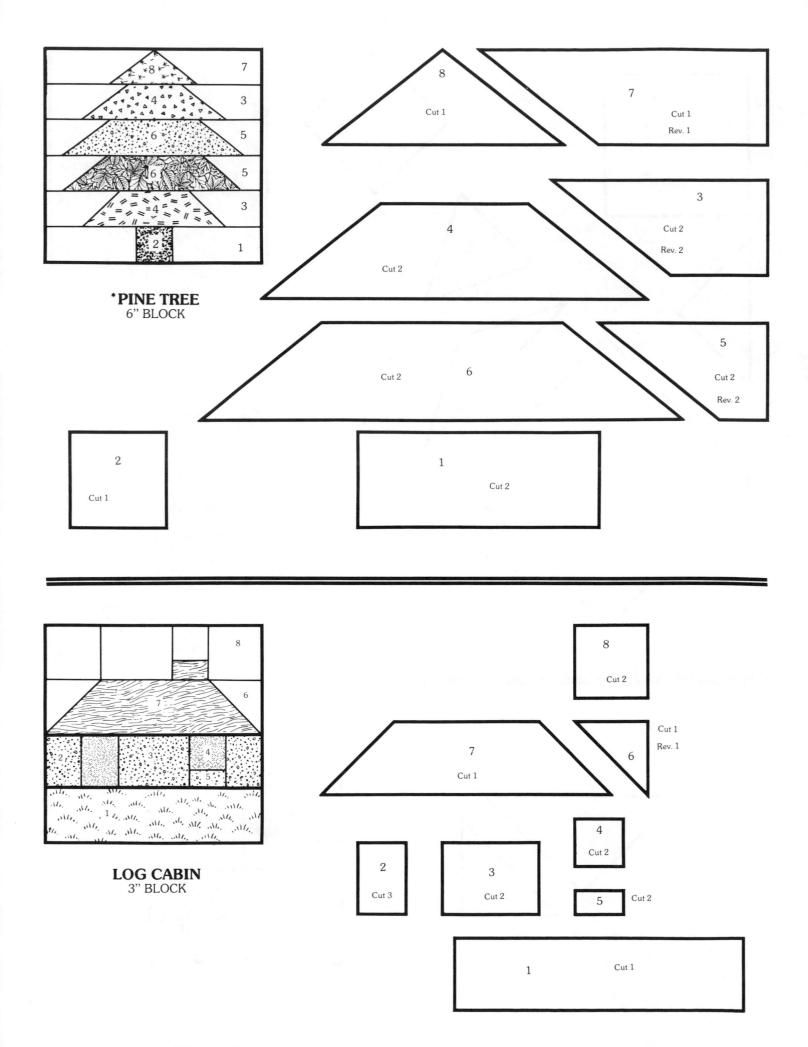

*PINE TREE
6" BLOCK

LOG CABIN
3" BLOCK

Add Seam Allowance

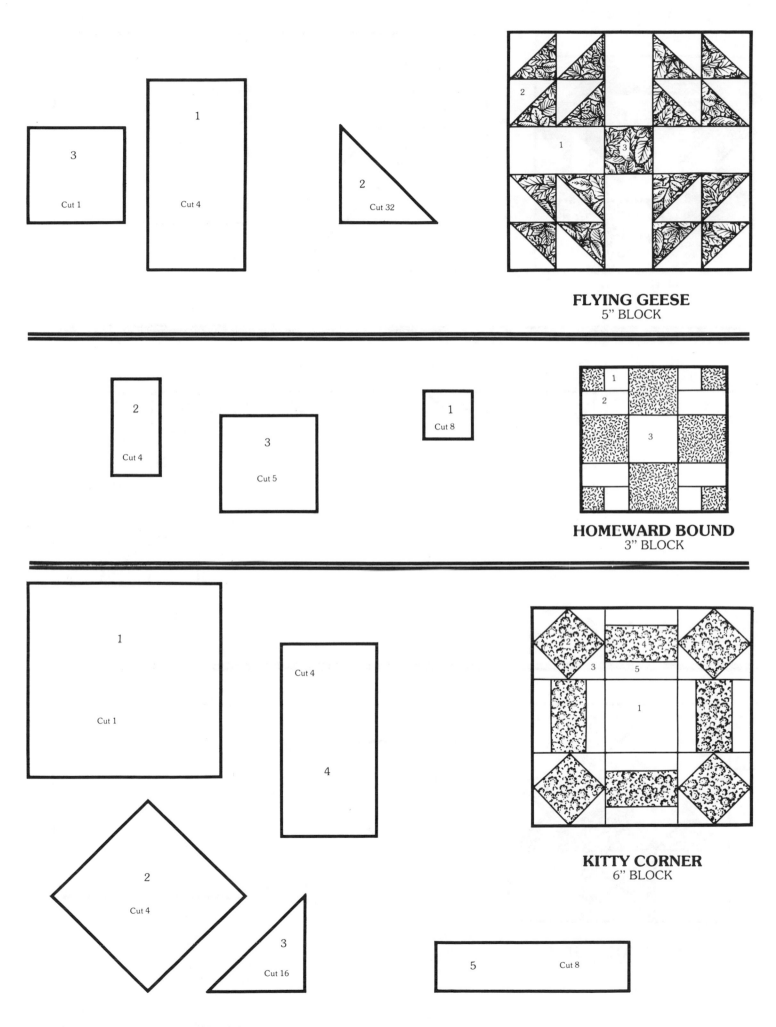

3

Cut 1

1

Cut 4

2

Cut 32

FLYING GEESE
5" BLOCK

2

Cut 4

3

Cut 5

1

Cut 8

HOMEWARD BOUND
3" BLOCK

1

Cut 1

Cut 4

4

2

Cut 4

3

Cut 16

5   Cut 8

KITTY CORNER
6" BLOCK

Add Seam Allowance

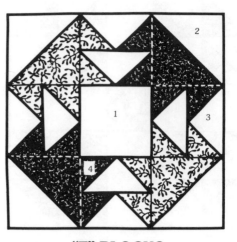

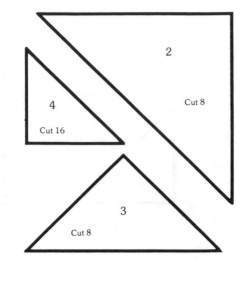

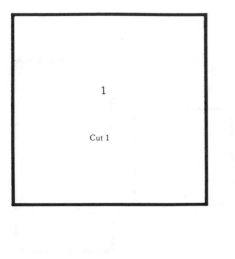

"T" BLOCKS
6" BLOCK

2

4
Cut 16

2
Cut 8

3
Cut 8

1
Cut 1

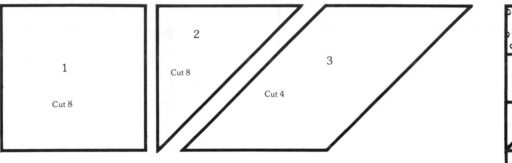

1
Cut 8

2
Cut 8

3
Cut 4

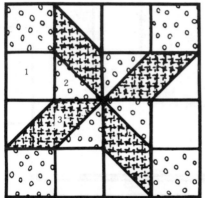

1

2

3

CLAY'S CHOICE
6" BLOCK

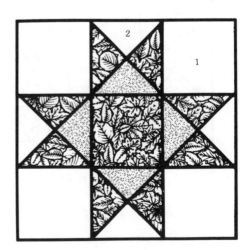

2

1

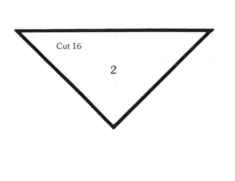

Cut 16

2

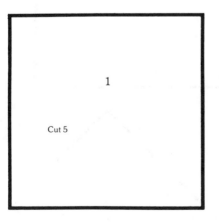

1
Cut 5

EIGHT POINT STAR
6" BLOCK

Add Seam Allowance

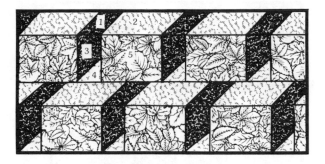

*ILLUSION
4¾" REPEAT

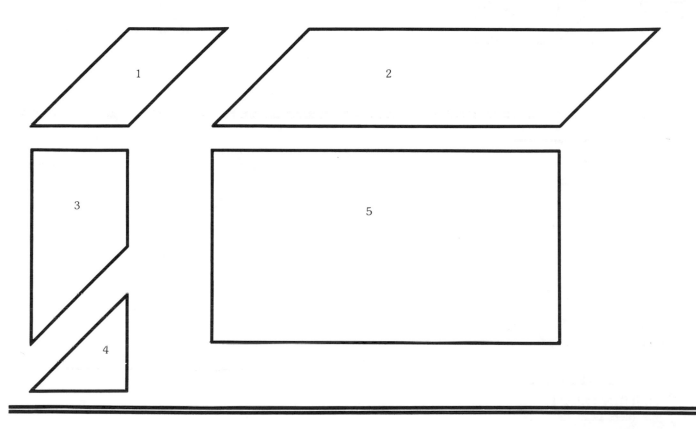

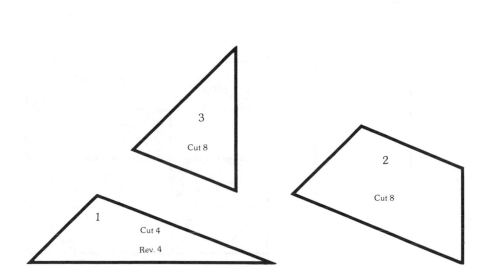

Add Seam Allowance

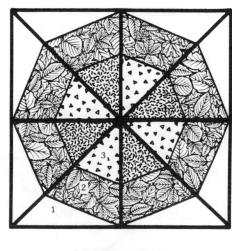

SPIDER WEB
5" BLOCK

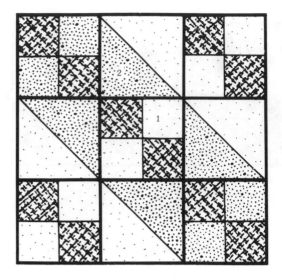

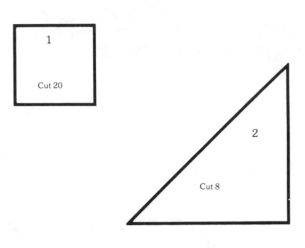

JACOB'S LADDER
5" BLOCK

1
Cut 20

2
Cut 8

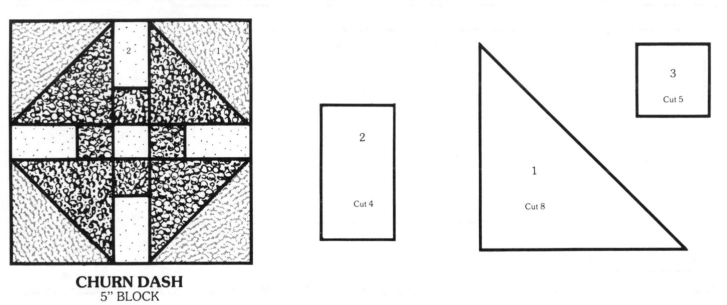

CHURN DASH
5" BLOCK

3
Cut 5

2
Cut 4

1
Cut 8

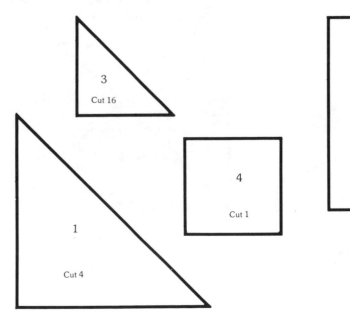

3
Cut 16

2
Cut 4

4
Cut 1

1
Cut 4

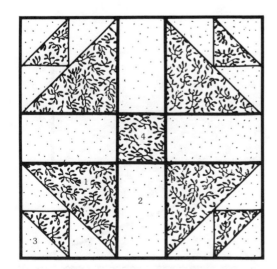

CORN AND BEANS
5" BLOCK

Add Seam Allowance

30

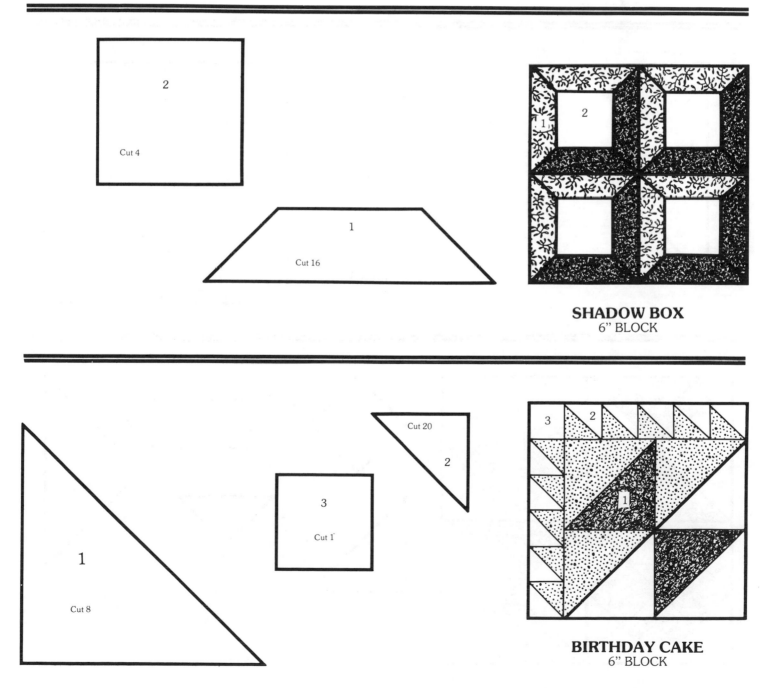

DAVID AND GOLIATH
5" BLOCK

3
Cut 13

Cut 8
4

2
Cut 4

1
Cut 8
Rev. 8

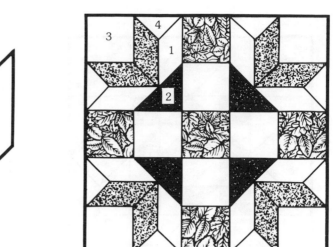

SHADOW BOX
6" BLOCK

2
Cut 4

1
Cut 16

BIRTHDAY CAKE
6" BLOCK

Cut 20
2

3
Cut 1

1
Cut 8

Add Seam Allowance

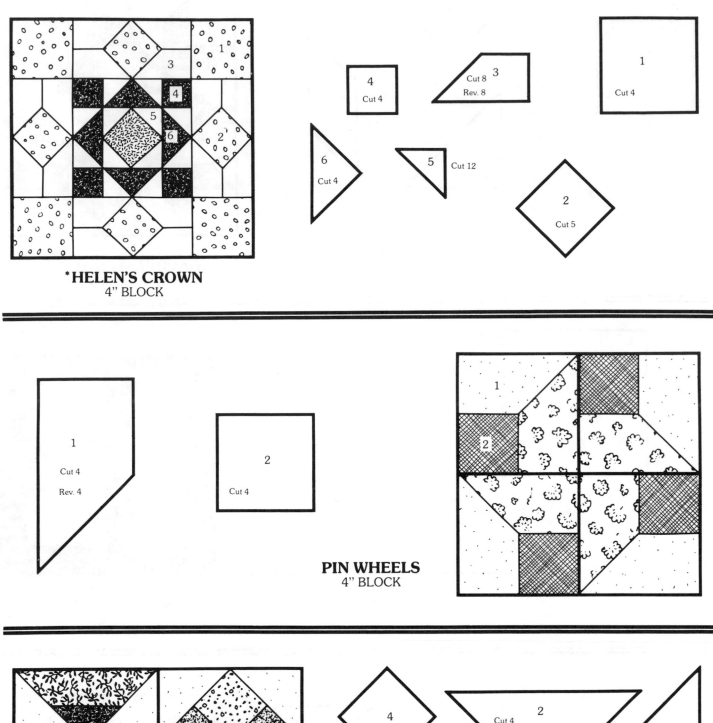

*HELEN'S CROWN
4" BLOCK

4
Cut 4

Cut 8 3
Rev. 8

1
Cut 4

6
Cut 4

5   Cut 12

2
Cut 5

1
Cut 4
Rev. 4

2
Cut 4

PIN WHEELS
4" BLOCK

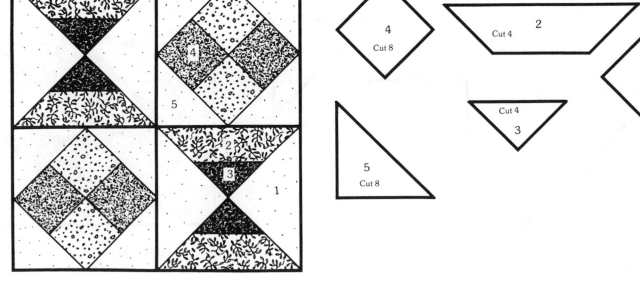

CONVENTIONAL BLOCK
4" BLOCK

4
Cut 8

2
Cut 4

1
Cut 4

Cut 4
3

5
Cut 8

Add Seam Allowance

Plate 1.   Star Within a Star Quilt by Gay Imbach. 6" Blocks. Soft Box by Nancy Downs. 4" Blocks.

Plate 2.   Infant Seat Cover and Album Quilt by Gay Imbach. 5" and 6" Blocks. Doll and Dress by Sharon Joor. 1" Border.

Plate 3. Wall Hangings by Gay Imbach. 6" Blocks.

Plate 4.   Chair Cushions and Lamp Shade by Shannon Newton. 5" Blocks. Wall Hanging and Magazine Rack by Gay Imbach. 6", 4" Blocks.

Plate 5.   Doll and Dress by Joan Aasen. 3" Block.

Plate 6.   Sampler Quilt by Gay Imbach. 6" Blocks.

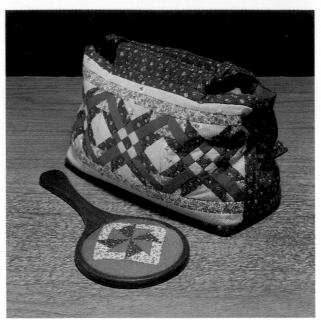

Plate 7.   Purse and Mirror by Gay Imbach. 4", and 3" Blocks.

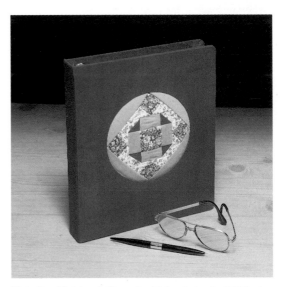

Plate 8.   Notebook Cover by Helen Imbach. 4" Block.

Plate 9.   Wall Quilt by Nancy Brosious.
            Bell Pull by Shannon Newton.
            Doll and Dress by Joan Aasen.
            Christmas Tree Ornaments by Gay Imbach. 3" and 6"
            Blocks.

Plate 10.   Rocking Chair Cushions by Joan Womack. 6" Blocks.

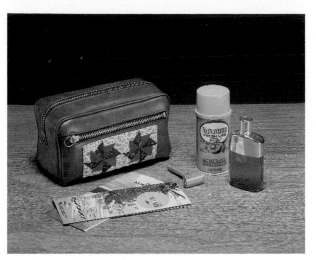

Plate 11.   Shaving Kit by Gay Imbach. 3" Blocks.

Plate 12.   Wall Hanging by Joan Aasen. 3" Blocks.

Plate 13.   Humidor, Tissue Box Cover and Pen Set by Gay Imbach. 3" Blocks. Tie by Joyce Bacon. 3" Block.

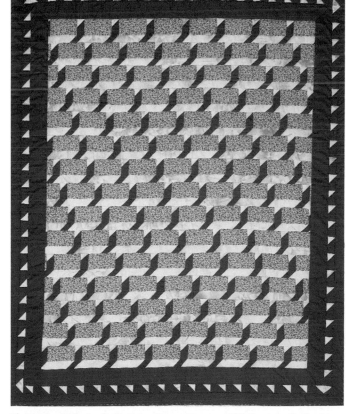

Plate 14.   "Illusion" Quilt by Joyce Bacon. 4¾" Repeat. Quilted by Edith Ehresman.

Plate 15.   Magazine Rack by Gay Imbach. 4" Blocks.

Plate 16. Sampler Quilt by Gay Imbach. 5" Blocks.

Plate 17. Sampler Quilt by Nancy Brosious. 6" Blocks.

Plate 18. Picnic Quilt and Basket by Gay Imbach. 5" Blocks and 2" Border.

Plate 19.   FEATHERED STAR MEDALLION by Gay Imbach.
The borders utilize 3," 5" and 6" patchwork.

Plate 20.   Pillows by Nancy Brosious. 4", 5" and 6" Blocks.

Plate 21.   Needles Eye by Joyce Bacon.
            Quilted by Gay Imbach.

Plate 22.   Planter, Picture Frame and
            children by Gay Imbach.
            3" Blocks.

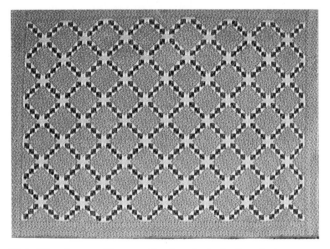

Plate 23.   Antique Miniature Patchwork. Author's collection.
            Border Pattern 16.

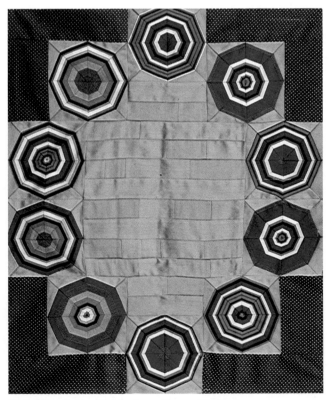

Plate 24.   Spider Web by Joyce Bacon. 5" Blocks.

Plate 25.   Sampler Quilt by Joan Aasen. 6" Blocks.

Plate 26.   Serving Tray by Gay Imbach. 5" Block.

Plate 27.   Jewelry Box by Gay Imbach. 3" Block.

Plate 28.   Note Book Covers by Helen Imbach. 3", 4" and 5" Blocks.

Plate 29.   Sampler Wall Hanging by Nancy Downs. 4" Blocks.

Plate 31. Patchwork Vest by Gay Imbach. 5" Blocks.

Plate 30. Mother—Daughter Tunics by Gay Imbach. 6" and 3" Blocks. Modeled by Janice and Elisha Toth.

Plate 32. Patchwork Skirt by Joan Womack. 4" Blocks.

Plate 33. Child's Dresses by Gay Imbach. 6," 5" and 3" Blocks.

Plate 34. Patchwork Vest by Wanda Belcher. 5" Blocks.

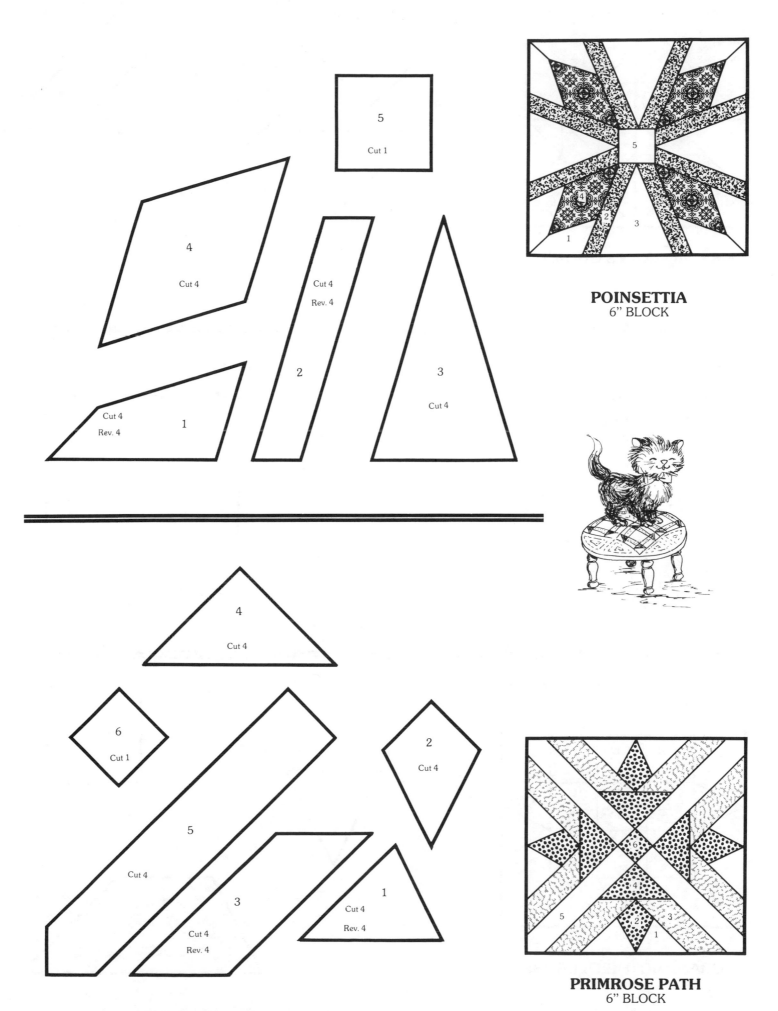

5

Cut 1

4

Cut 4

Cut 4
Rev. 4

2

3

Cut 4

Cut 4
Rev. 4

1

POINSETTIA
6" BLOCK

4

Cut 4

6

Cut 1

2

Cut 4

5

Cut 4

3

Cut 4
Rev. 4

1

Cut 4
Rev. 4

PRIMROSE PATH
6" BLOCK

Add Seam Allowance

41

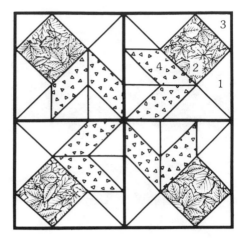

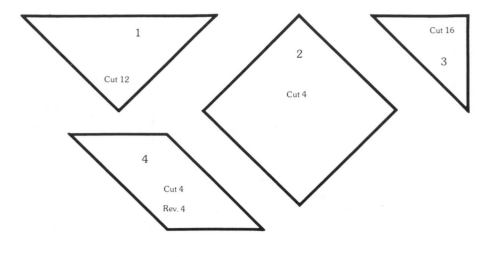

MRS. MORGAN'S CHOICE
6" BLOCK

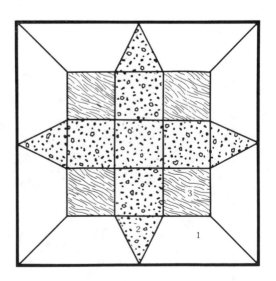

SLASHED ALBUM
4" BLOCK

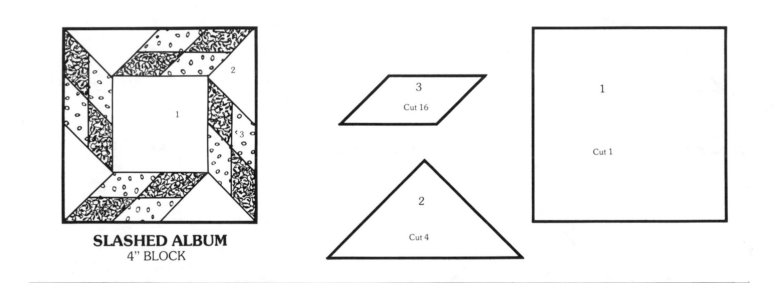

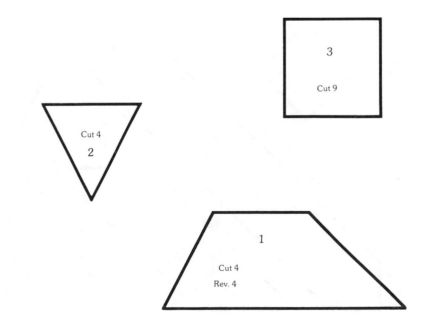

GRANDMOTHER'S CROSS
5" BLOCK

Add Seam Allowance

42

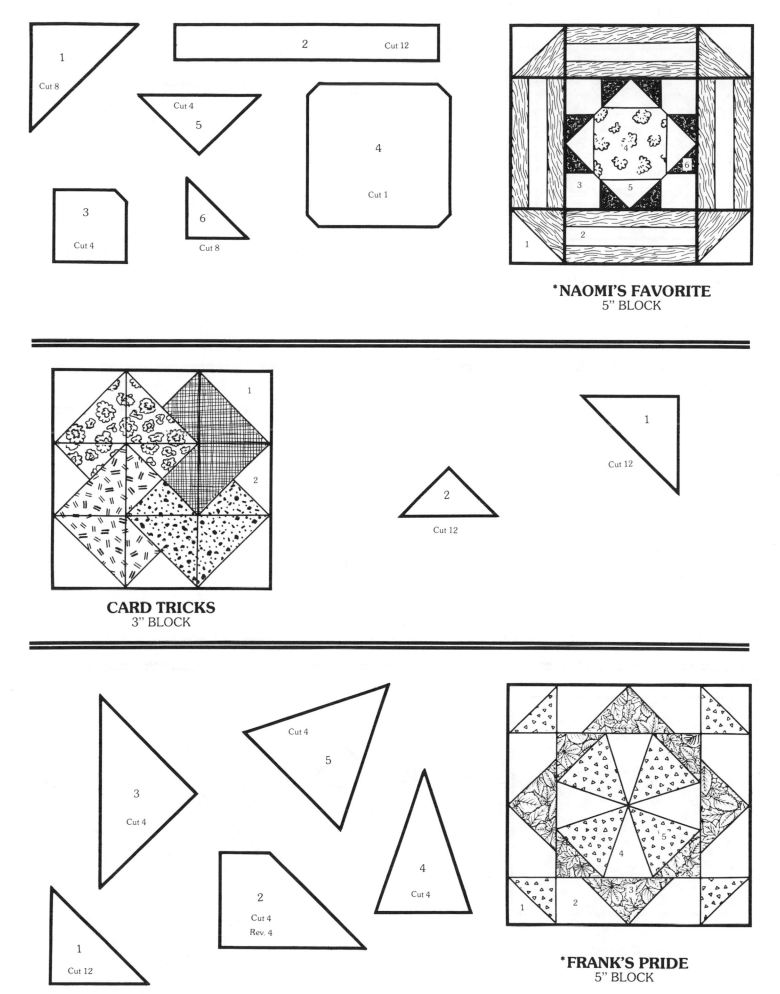

1
Cut 8

2   Cut 12

Cut 4
5

4

Cut 1

3
Cut 4

6
Cut 8

*NAOMI'S FAVORITE
5" BLOCK

CARD TRICKS
3" BLOCK

1
Cut 12

2
Cut 12

3
Cut 4

Cut 4
5

4
Cut 4

1
Cut 12

2
Cut 4
Rev. 4

*FRANK'S PRIDE
5" BLOCK

Add Seam Allowance

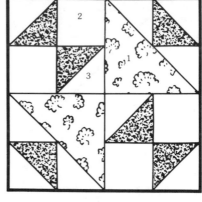

ROCKY MOUNTAIN PUZZLE

4" BLOCK

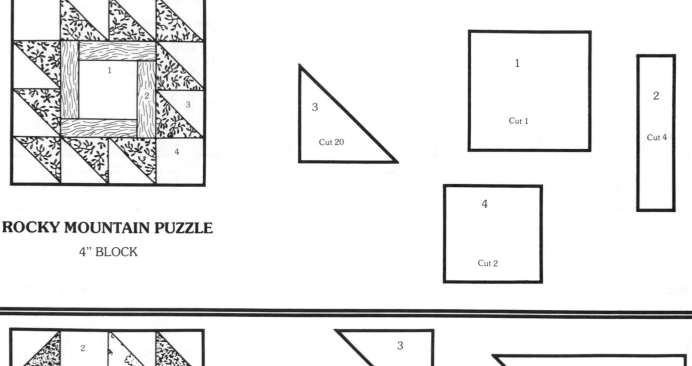

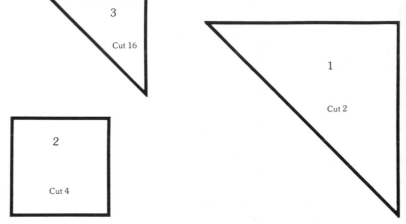

CROSSES AND LOSSES
4" BLOCK

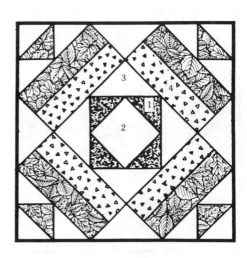

* LEVI'S DOMAIN
3" BLOCK

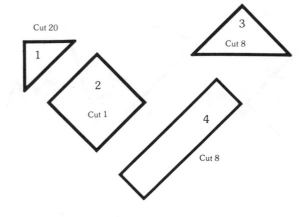

Add Seam Allowance

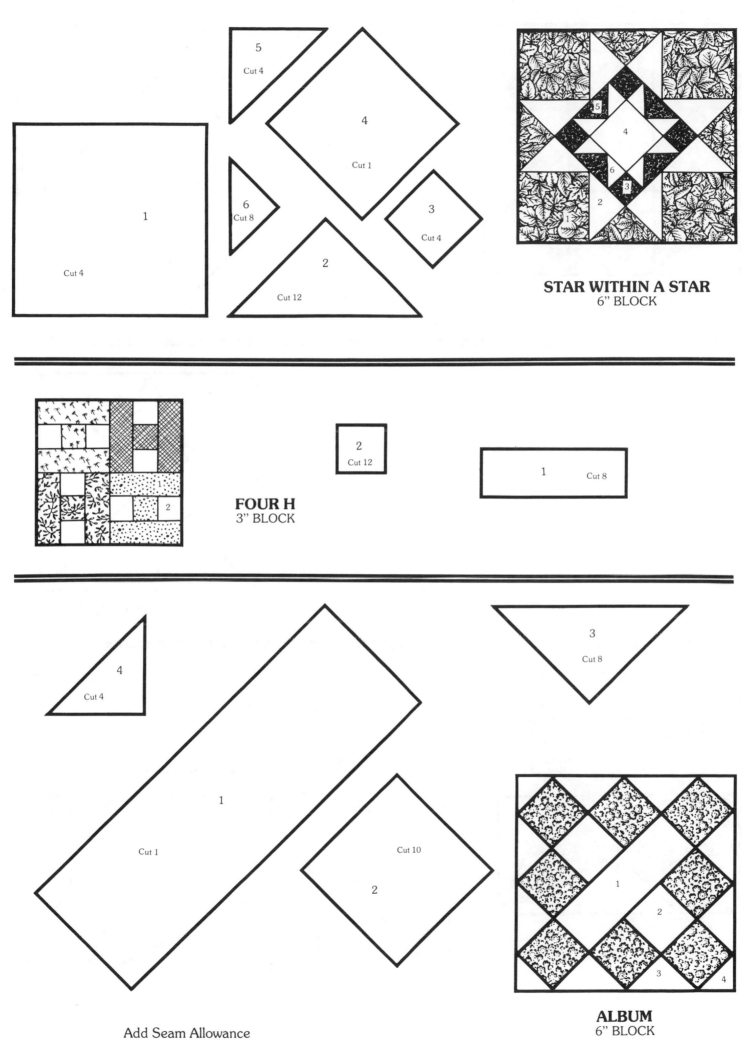

5
Cut 4

1
Cut 4

4
Cut 1

6
Cut 8

3
Cut 4

2
Cut 12

STAR WITHIN A STAR
6" BLOCK

2
Cut 12

1
Cut 8

FOUR H
3" BLOCK

3
Cut 8

4
Cut 4

1
Cut 1

2
Cut 10

ALBUM
6" BLOCK

Add Seam Allowance

45

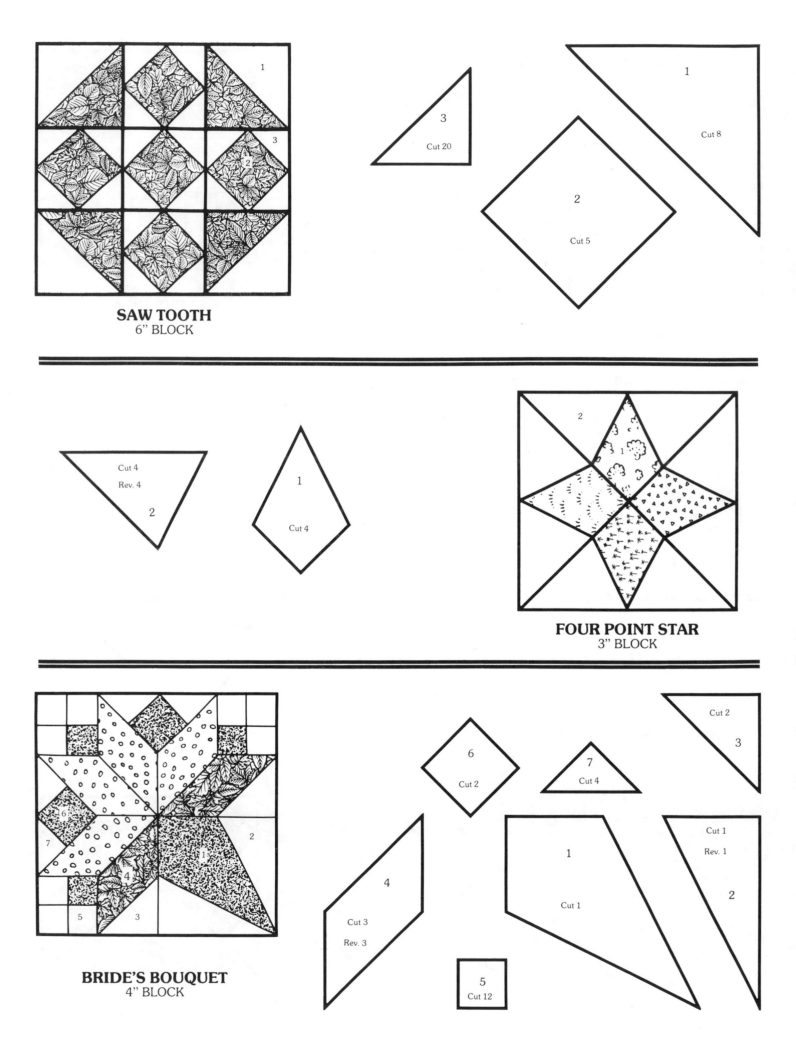

SAW TOOTH
6" BLOCK

1

3

2

3

Cut 20

1

Cut 8

2

Cut 5

Cut 4
Rev. 4

2

1

Cut 4

2

1

FOUR POINT STAR
3" BLOCK

Cut 2

3

6

Cut 2

7

Cut 4

Cut 1
Rev. 1

1

Cut 1

2

4

Cut 3
Rev. 3

5

Cut 12

BRIDE'S BOUQUET
4" BLOCK

6

7

2

4

5

3

1

Add Seam Allowance

46

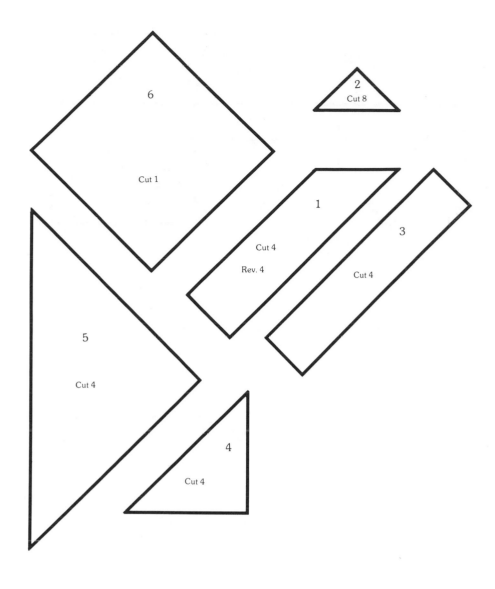

6
Cut 1

2
Cut 8

1
Cut 4
Rev. 4

3
Cut 4

5
Cut 4

4
Cut 4

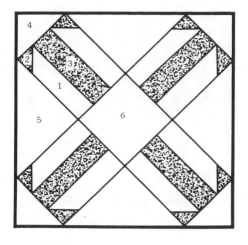

BOXED T'S
6" BLOCK

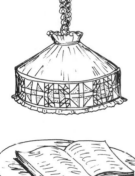

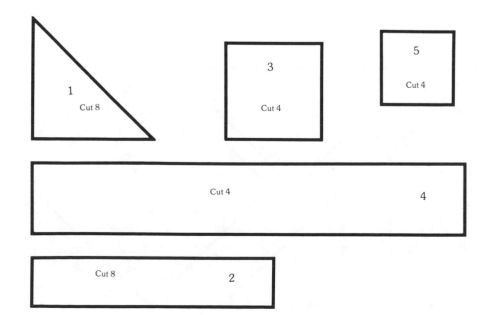

1
Cut 8

3
Cut 4

5
Cut 4

4
Cut 4

2
Cut 8

Add Seam Allowance

*MONTEREY
6" BLOCK

47

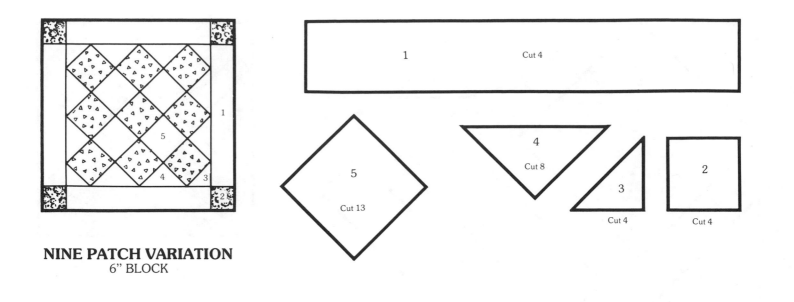

NINE PATCH VARIATION
6" BLOCK

1   Cut 4

5   Cut 13

4   Cut 8

3   Cut 4

2   Cut 4

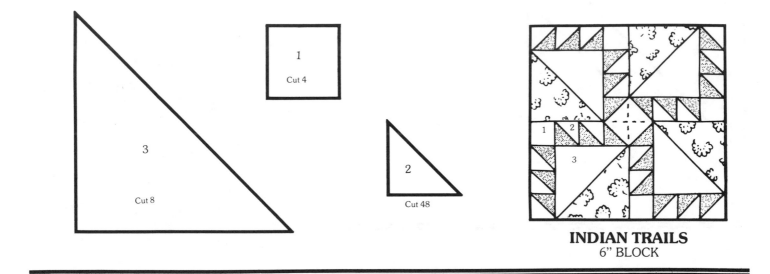

3   Cut 8

1   Cut 4

2   Cut 48

INDIAN TRAILS
6" BLOCK

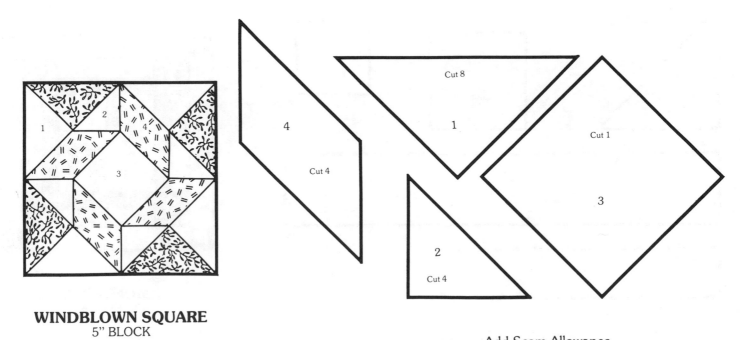

WINDBLOWN SQUARE
5" BLOCK

Cut 8

4   Cut 4

1

Cut 1

3

2   Cut 4

Add Seam Allowance

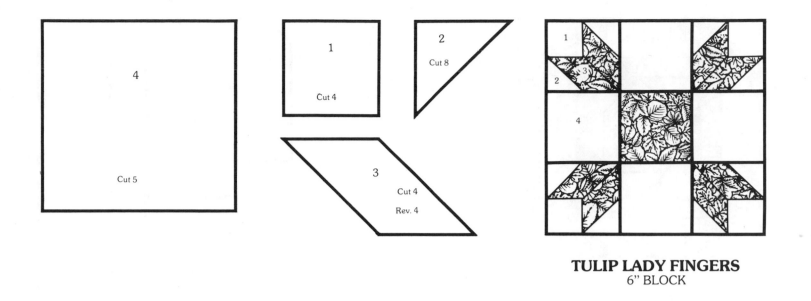

TULIP LADY FINGERS
6" BLOCK

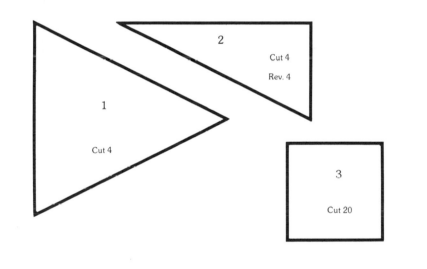

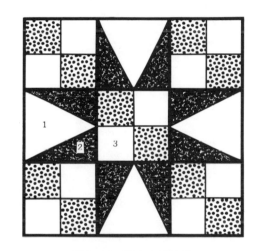

54-40 OR FIGHT
6" BLOCK

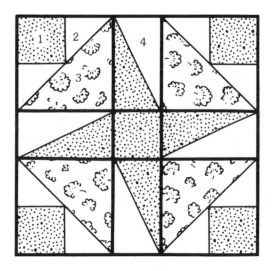

CRAZY ANN
5" BLOCK

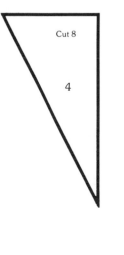

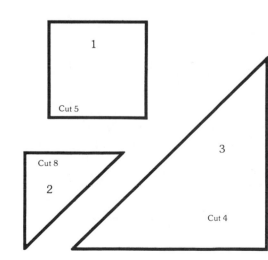

Add Seam Allowance

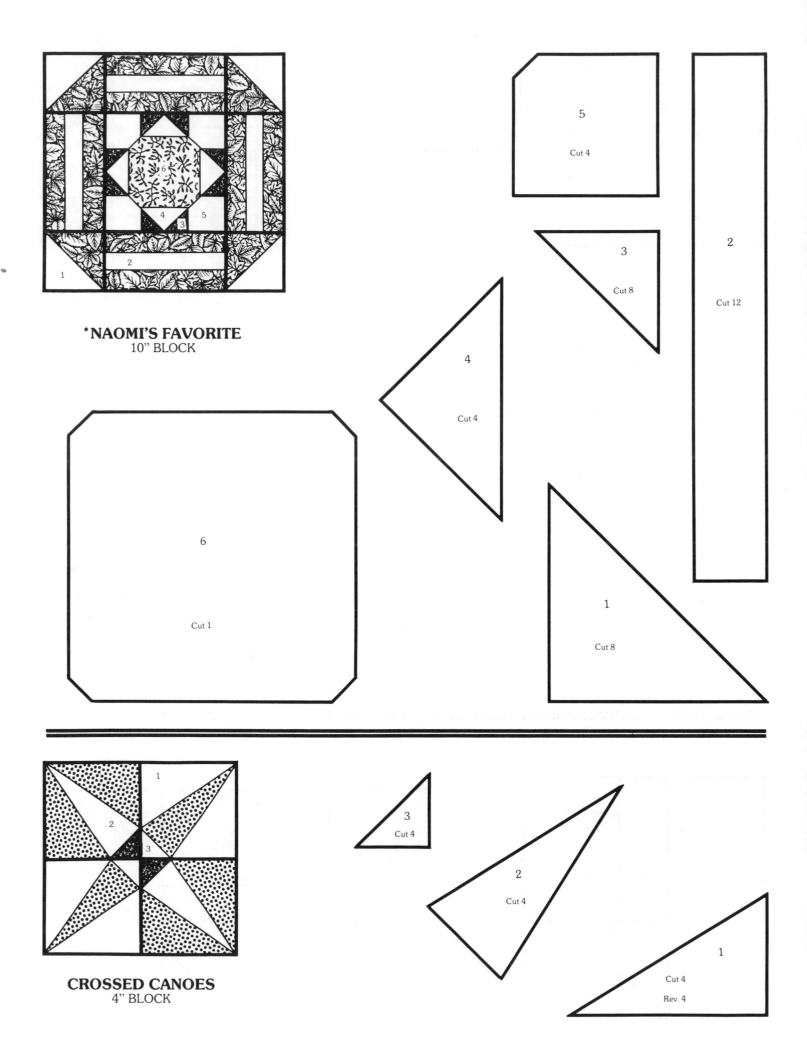

*NAOMI'S FAVORITE
10" BLOCK

5
Cut 4

3
Cut 8

2
Cut 12

4
Cut 4

6
Cut 1

1
Cut 8

CROSSED CANOES
4" BLOCK

3
Cut 4

2
Cut 4

1
Cut 4
Rev. 4

Add Seam Allowance

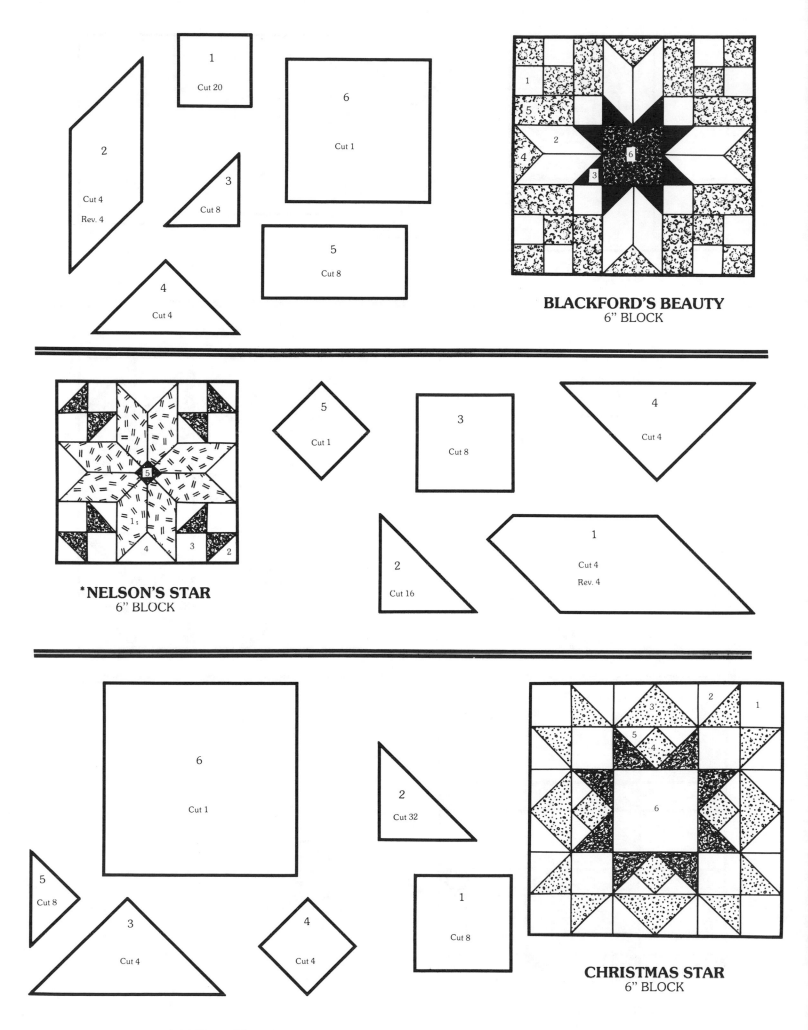

1

Cut 20

2

Cut 4
Rev. 4

3

Cut 8

6

Cut 1

5

Cut 8

4

Cut 4

1

5

2

4

6

3

BLACKFORD'S BEAUTY
6" BLOCK

*NELSON'S STAR
6" BLOCK

5

Cut 1

3

Cut 8

4

Cut 4

2

Cut 16

1

Cut 4
Rev. 4

6

Cut 1

2

Cut 32

5

Cut 8

3

Cut 4

4

Cut 4

1

Cut 8

3

5

4

2

1

6

CHRISTMAS STAR
6" BLOCK

Add Seam Allowance

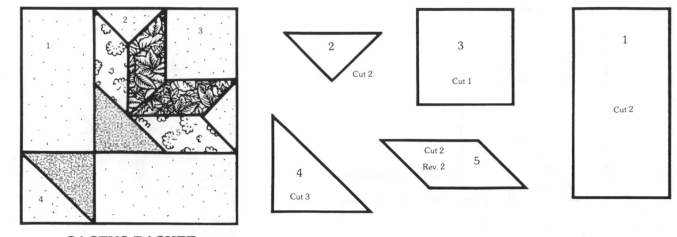

CACTUS BASKET
3" BLOCK

2 Cut 2

3 Cut 1

1 Cut 2

4 Cut 3

Cut 2 Rev. 2

5

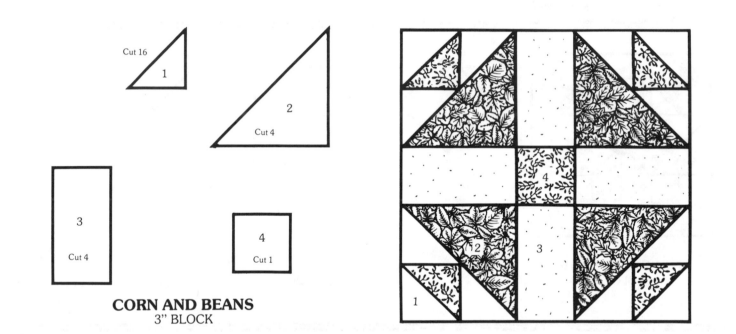

Cut 16 1

2 Cut 4

3 Cut 4

4 Cut 1

CORN AND BEANS
3" BLOCK

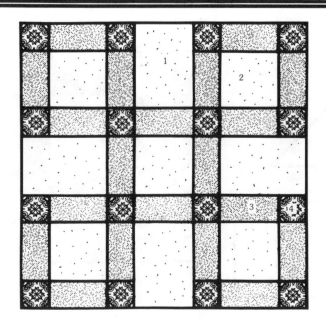

STRIPES AND SQUARES
3" BLOCK

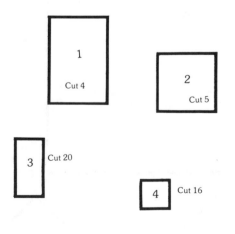

1 Cut 4

2 Cut 5

3 Cut 20

4 Cut 16

Add Seam Allowance

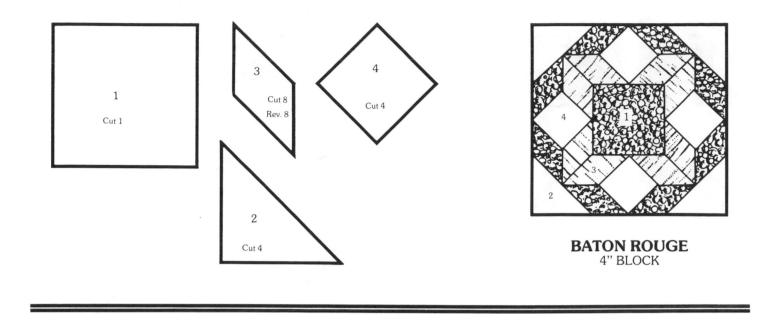

1
Cut 1

3
Cut 8
Rev. 8

4
Cut 4

2
Cut 4

BATON ROUGE
4" BLOCK

3
Cut 8

2
Cut 8

1
Cut 1

BARN DOOR
4" BLOCK

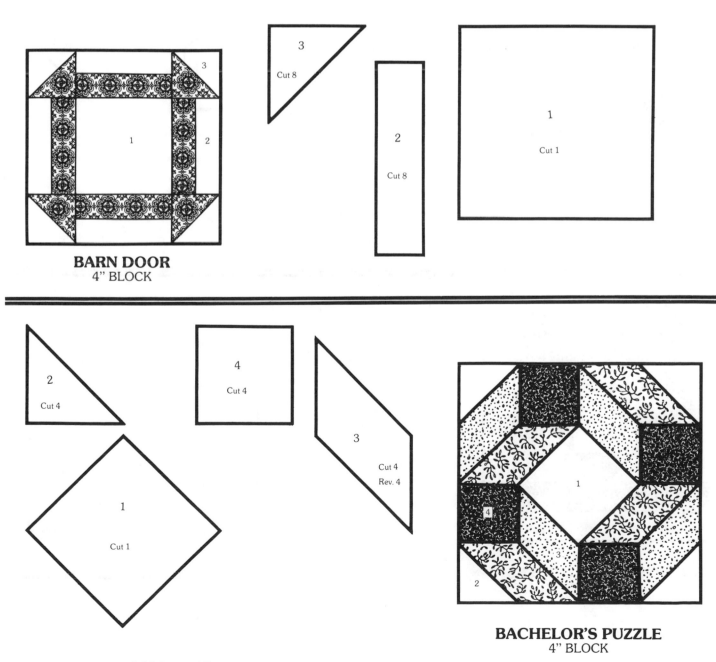

2
Cut 4

4
Cut 4

3
Cut 4
Rev. 4

1
Cut 1

BACHELOR'S PUZZLE
4" BLOCK

Add Seam Allowance

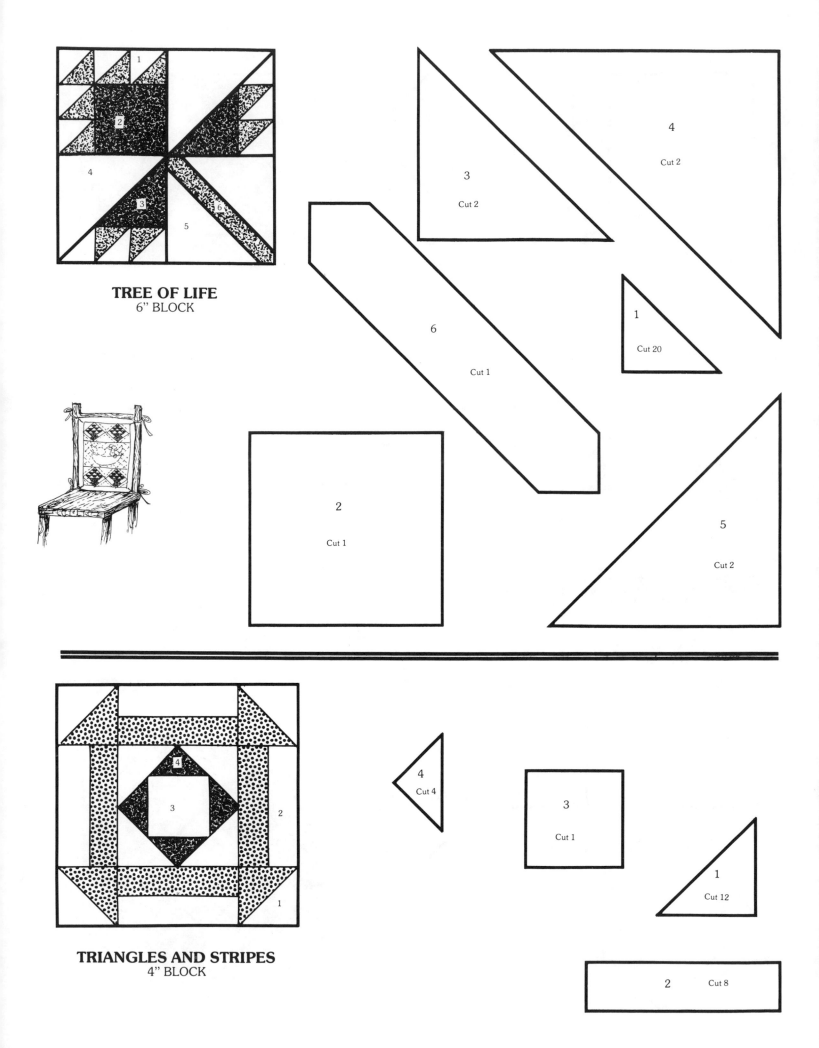

TREE OF LIFE
6" BLOCK

1

2

3
Cut 2

4
Cut 2

6
Cut 1

1
Cut 20

2
Cut 1

5
Cut 2

TRIANGLES AND STRIPES
4" BLOCK

4
Cut 4

3
Cut 1

1
Cut 12

2   Cut 8

Add Seam Allowance

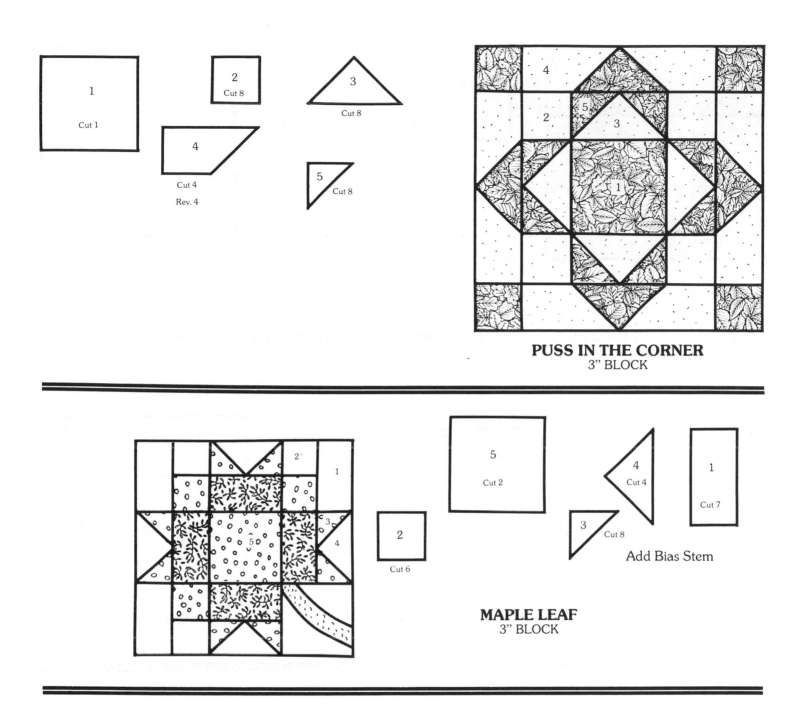

1
Cut 1

2
Cut 8

3
Cut 8

4
Cut 4
Rev. 4

5
Cut 8

PUSS IN THE CORNER
3" BLOCK

5
Cut 2

2
Cut 6

4
Cut 4

3
Cut 8

1
Cut 7

Add Bias Stem

MAPLE LEAF
3" BLOCK

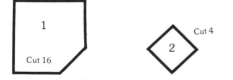

1
Cut 16

2
Cut 4

Add Seam Allowance

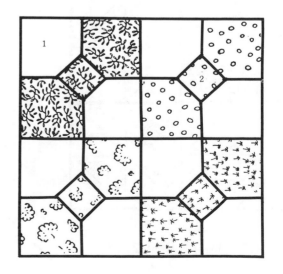

BOW TIE
3" BLOCK

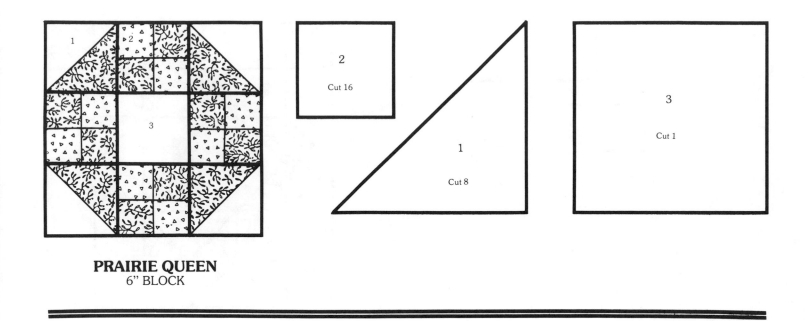

PRAIRIE QUEEN
6" BLOCK

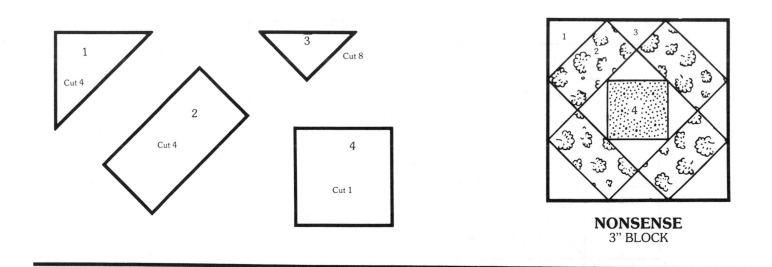

NONSENSE
3" BLOCK

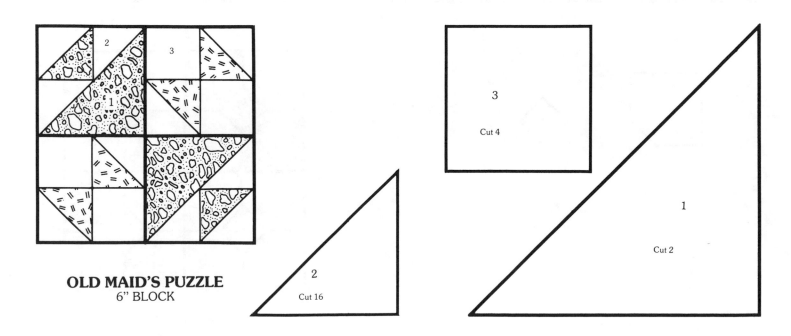

OLD MAID'S PUZZLE
6" BLOCK

Add Seam Allowance

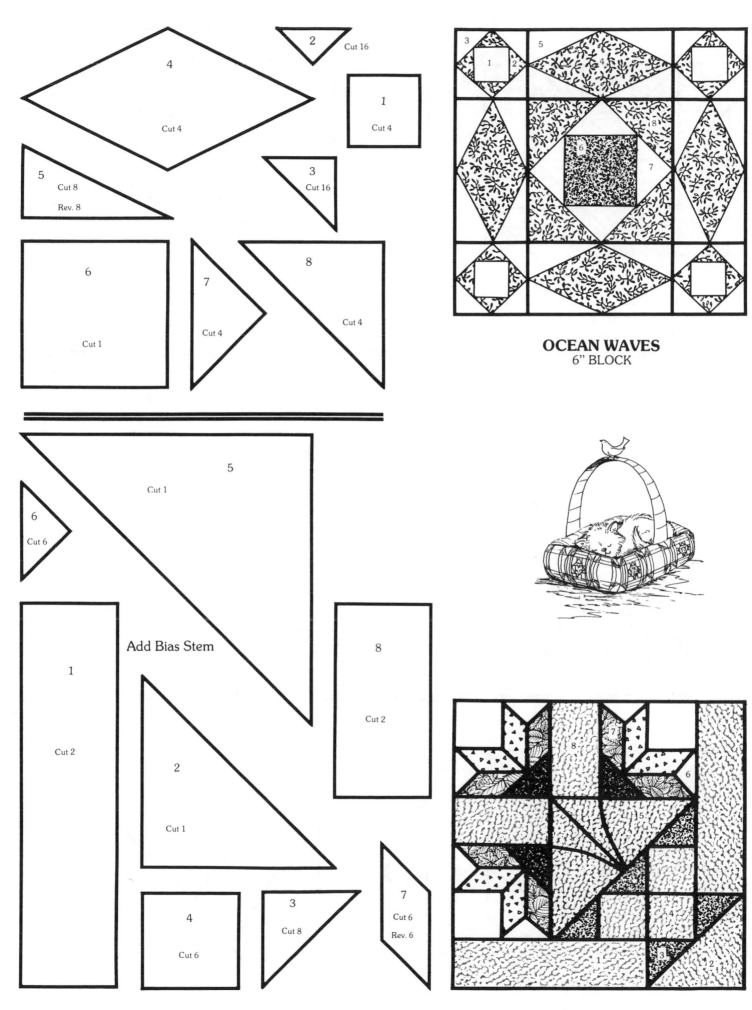

4

Cut 4

2

Cut 16

1

Cut 4

5

Cut 8

Rev. 8

3

Cut 16

6

Cut 1

7

Cut 4

8

Cut 4

OCEAN WAVES
6" BLOCK

5

Cut 1

6

Cut 6

Add Bias Stem

1

Cut 2

8

Cut 2

2

Cut 1

4

Cut 6

3

Cut 8

7

Cut 6

Rev. 6

Add Seam Allowance

BASKET OF LILIES
6" BLOCK

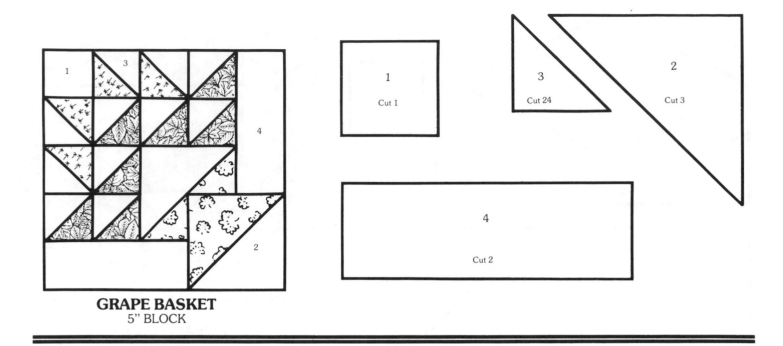

GRAPE BASKET
5" BLOCK

1
Cut 1

3
Cut 24

2
Cut 3

4
Cut 2

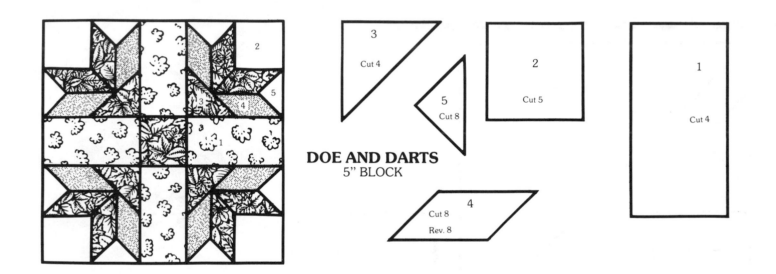

DOE AND DARTS
5" BLOCK

3
Cut 4

5
Cut 8

2
Cut 5

1
Cut 4

4
Cut 8
Rev. 8

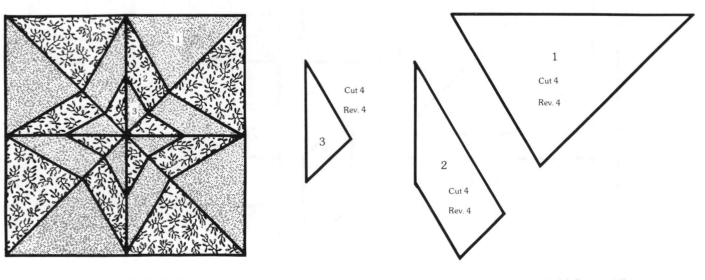

NIGHT AND DAY
5" BLOCK

3
Cut 4
Rev. 4

2
Cut 4
Rev. 4

1
Cut 4
Rev. 4

Add Seam Allowance

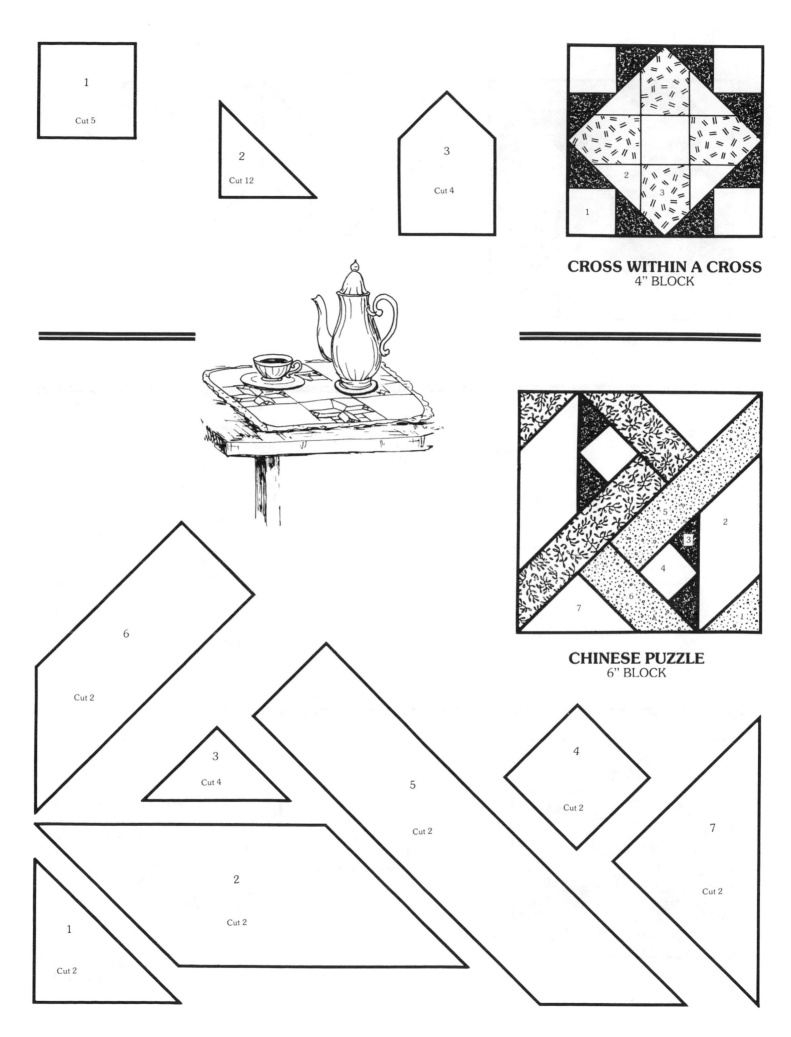

1

Cut 5

2

Cut 12

3

Cut 4

CROSS WITHIN A CROSS
4" BLOCK

2

3

1

CHINESE PUZZLE
6" BLOCK

5

2

3

4

6

7

1

6

Cut 2

3

Cut 4

5

Cut 2

4

Cut 2

7

Cut 2

2

Cut 2

1

Cut 2

Add Seam Allowance

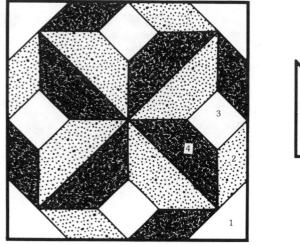
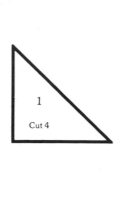
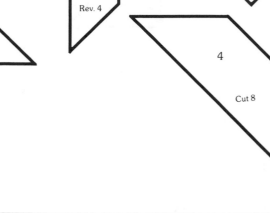

1
Cut 4

2
Cut 4
Rev. 4

3
Cut 4

4
Cut 8

SHADED TRAIL
4" BLOCK

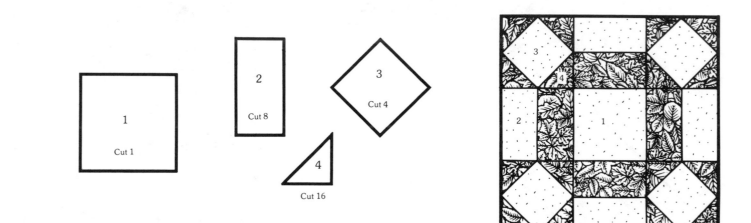

1
Cut 1

2
Cut 8

3
Cut 4

4
Cut 16

ROLLING STONE
3" BLOCK

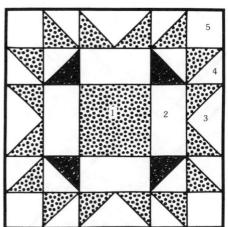
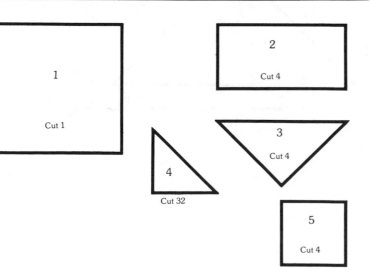

1
Cut 1

2
Cut 4

3
Cut 4

4
Cut 32

5
Cut 4

ROBBING PETER TO PAY PAUL
4" BLOCK

Add Seam Allowance

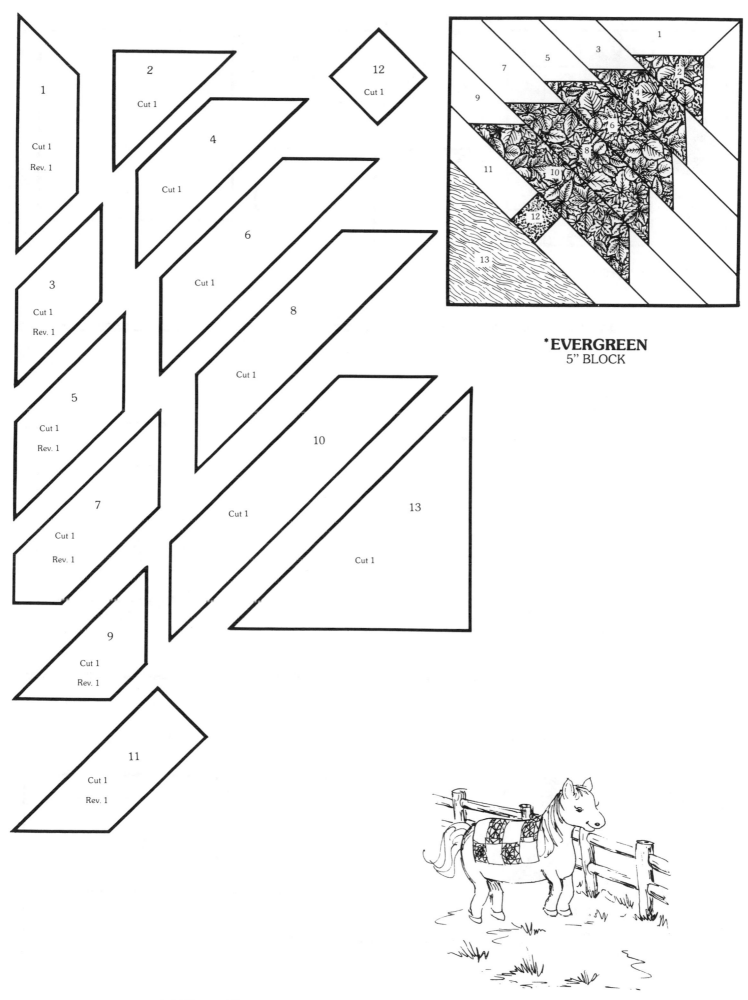

1

Cut 1
Rev. 1

2

Cut 1

4

Cut 1

3

Cut 1
Rev. 1

6

Cut 1

8

Cut 1

5

Cut 1
Rev. 1

7

Cut 1
Rev. 1

10

Cut 1

13

Cut 1

9

Cut 1
Rev. 1

11

Cut 1
Rev. 1

12

Cut 1

*EVERGREEN
5" BLOCK

Add Seam Allowance

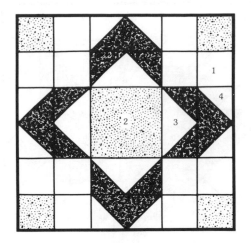

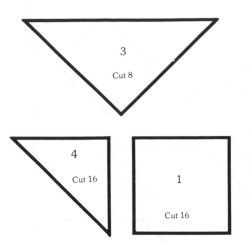

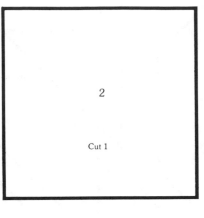

PUSS IN THE CORNER
6" BLOCK

3
Cut 8

4
Cut 16

1
Cut 16

2
Cut 1

ROLLING STONE
6" BLOCK

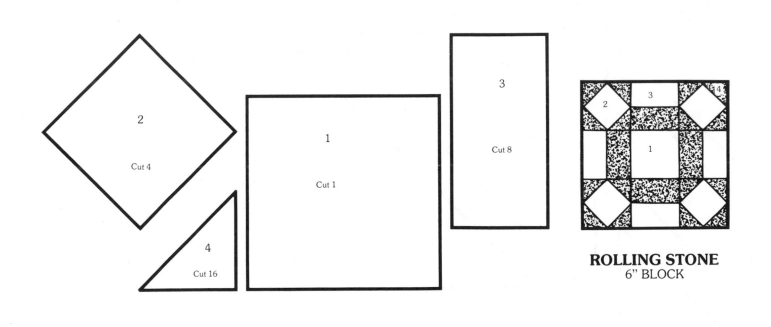

2
Cut 4

1
Cut 1

4
Cut 16

3
Cut 8

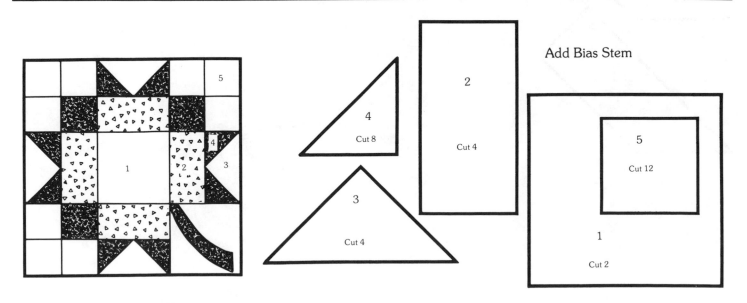

MAPLE LEAF
6" BLOCK

4
Cut 8

3
Cut 4

2
Cut 4

Add Bias Stem

5
Cut 12

1
Cut 2

Add Seam Allowance

1
Cut 7

3
Cut 2

2
Cut 28

CROWN OF THORNS
5" BLOCK

6
Cut 1

5   Cut 4

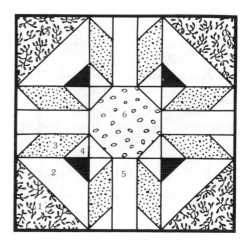

Cut 24

2
Cut 4

4

3
Cut 4
Rev. 4

1
Cut 4

Add Seam Allowance

MISS JACKSON
6" BLOCK

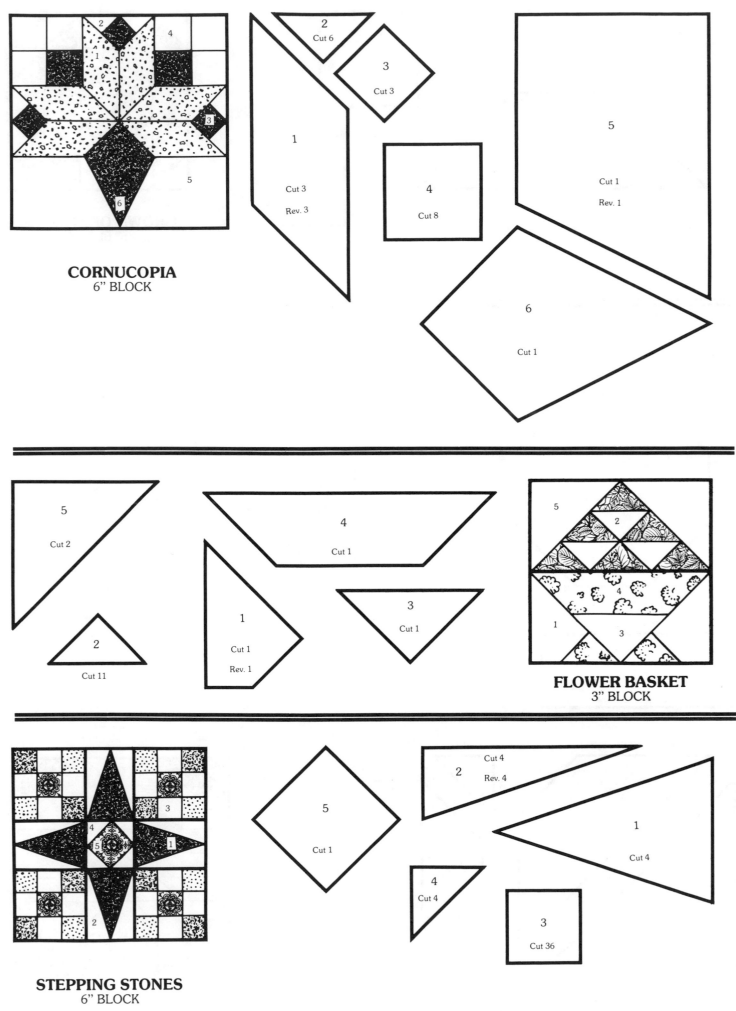

CORNUCOPIA
6" BLOCK

2
Cut 6

3
Cut 3

1
Cut 3
Rev. 3

4
Cut 8

5
Cut 1
Rev. 1

6
Cut 1

5
Cut 2

2
Cut 11

4
Cut 1

1
Cut 1
Rev. 1

3
Cut 1

FLOWER BASKET
3" BLOCK

STEPPING STONES
6" BLOCK

5
Cut 1

2
Cut 4
Rev. 4

1
Cut 4

4
Cut 4

3
Cut 36

Add Seam Allowance

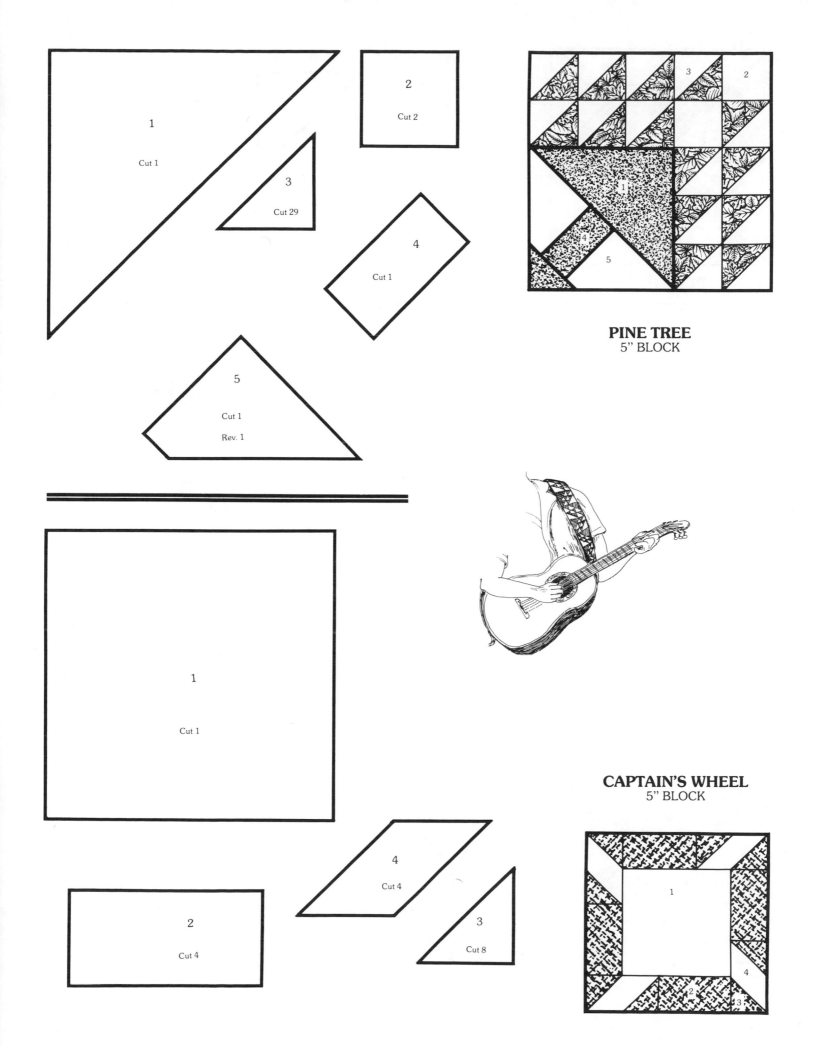

1

Cut 1

2

Cut 2

3

Cut 29

4

Cut 1

5

Cut 1

Rev. 1

PINE TREE
5" BLOCK

1

Cut 1

2

Cut 4

4

Cut 4

3

Cut 8

CAPTAIN'S WHEEL
5" BLOCK

Add Seam Allowance

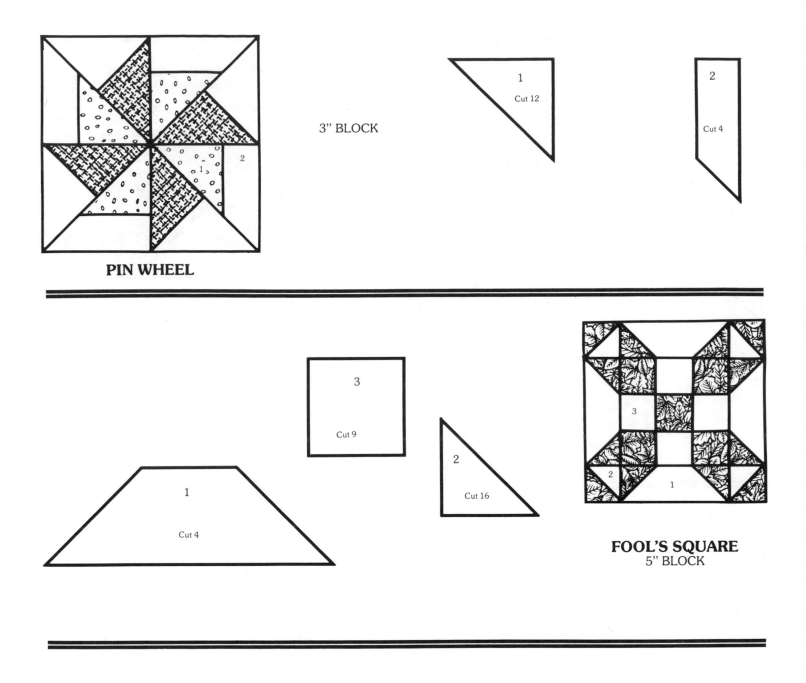

PIN WHEEL

3" BLOCK

1 Cut 12

2 Cut 4

3 Cut 9

1 Cut 4

2 Cut 16

FOOL'S SQUARE
5" BLOCK

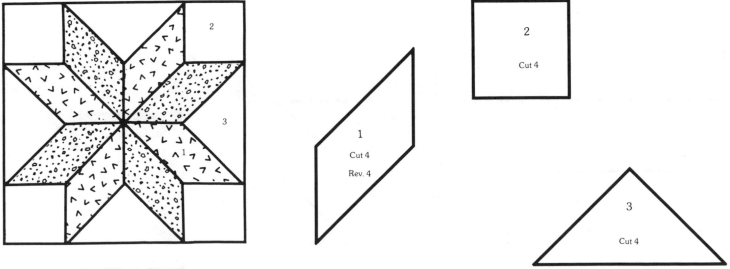

LEMOYNE STAR

4" BLOCK

2 Cut 4

1 Cut 4 Rev. 4

3 Cut 4

Add Seam Allowance

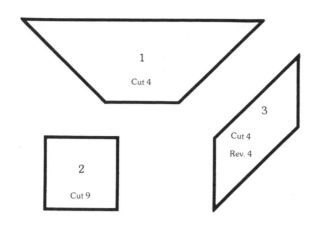

1
Cut 4

2
Cut 9

3
Cut 4
Rev. 4

4" BLOCK

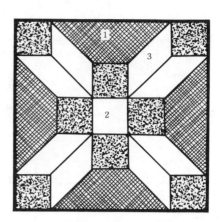

ROLLING STAR

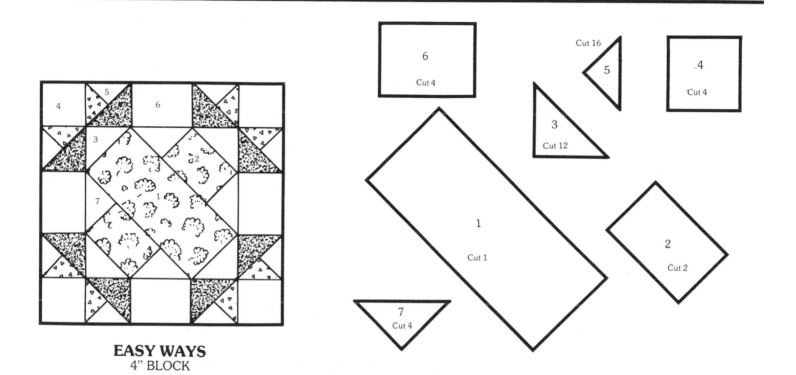

EASY WAYS
4" BLOCK

6
Cut 4

Cut 16

5

4
Cut 4

3
Cut 12

1
Cut 1

2
Cut 2

7
Cut 4

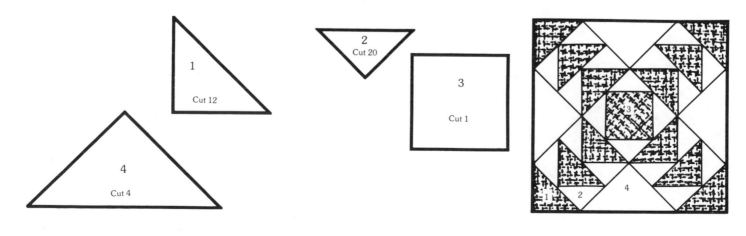

1
Cut 12

2
Cut 20

3
Cut 1

4
Cut 4

SPRING BEAUTY
4" BLOCK

Add Seam Allowance

67

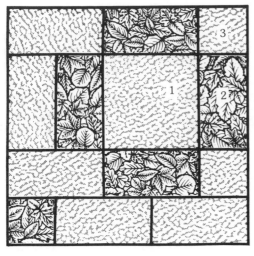

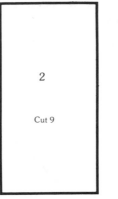

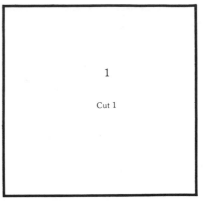

CHILDREN'S DELIGHT
5" BLOCK

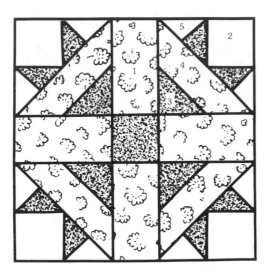

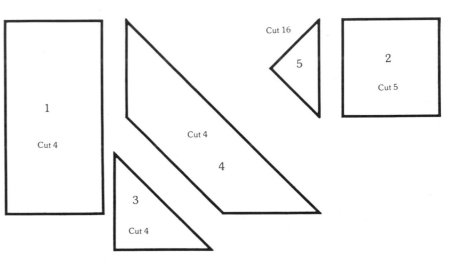

DAVID AND GOLIATH
5" BLOCK

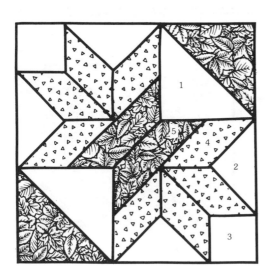

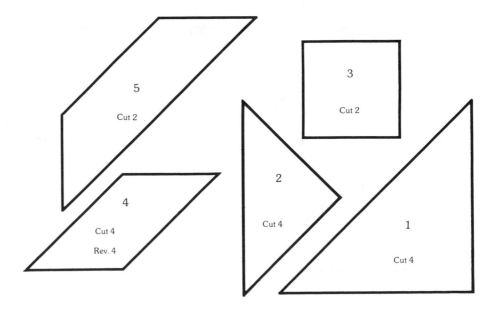

QUEEN CHARLOTTE'S CROWN
5" BLOCK

Add Seam Allowance

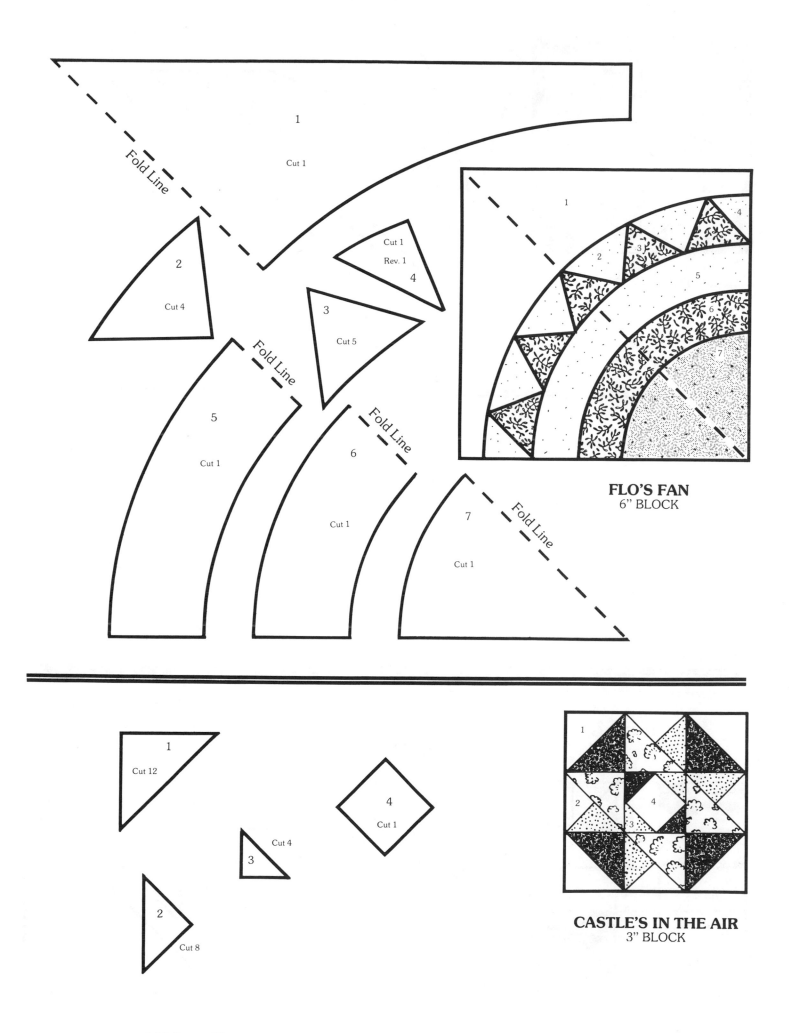

1

Cut 1

Fold Line

2

Cut 4

Fold Line

3

Cut 5

Cut 1
Rev. 1

4

Fold Line

5

Cut 1

6

Cut 1

Fold Line

7

Cut 1

Fold Line

1

2

3

4

5

6

7

FLO'S FAN
6" BLOCK

1

Cut 12

4

Cut 1

3

Cut 4

2

Cut 8

1

2

3

4

CASTLE'S IN THE AIR
3" BLOCK

Add Seam Allowance

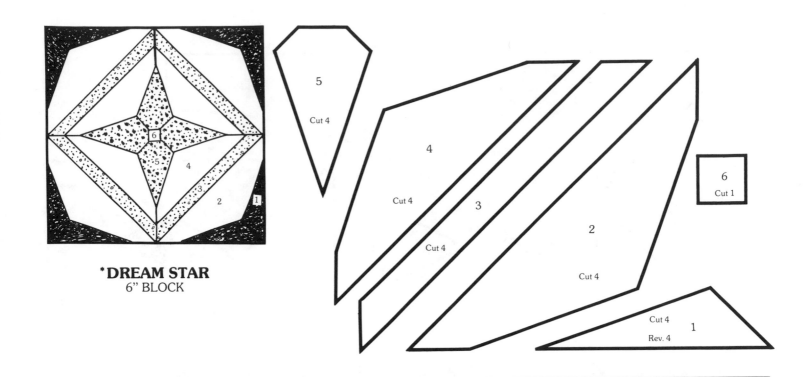

*DREAM STAR
6" BLOCK

5
Cut 4

4
Cut 4

3
Cut 4

2
Cut 4

6
Cut 1

1
Cut 4
Rev. 4

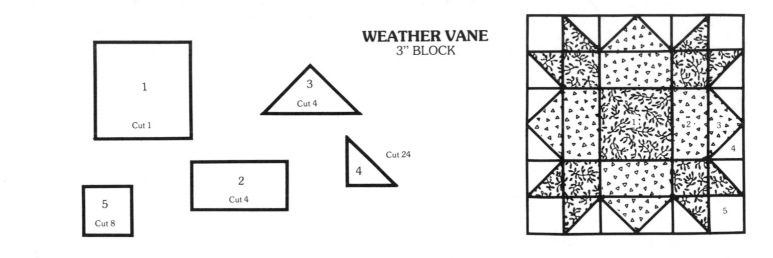

WEATHER VANE
3" BLOCK

1
Cut 1

3
Cut 4

2
Cut 4

5
Cut 8

4
Cut 24

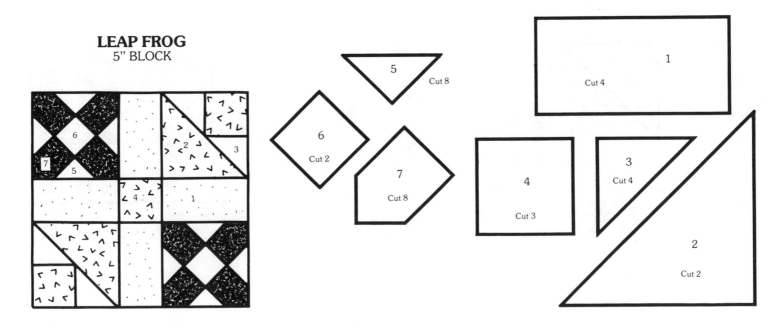

LEAP FROG
5" BLOCK

5
Cut 8

6
Cut 2

7
Cut 8

1
Cut 4

4
Cut 3

3
Cut 4

2
Cut 2

Add Seam Allowance

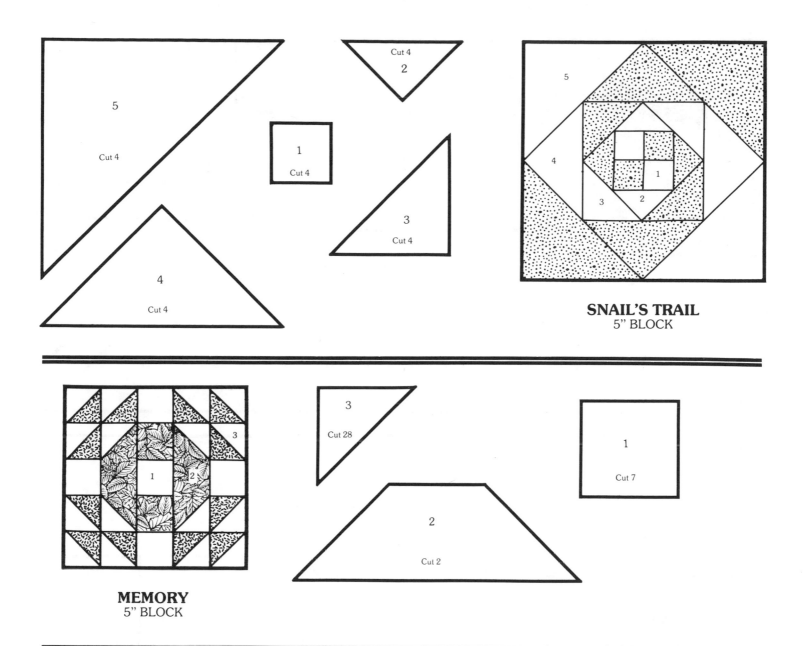

5
Cut 4

Cut 4
2

1
Cut 4

3
Cut 4

4
Cut 4

5
4
3
1
2

SNAIL'S TRAIL
5" BLOCK

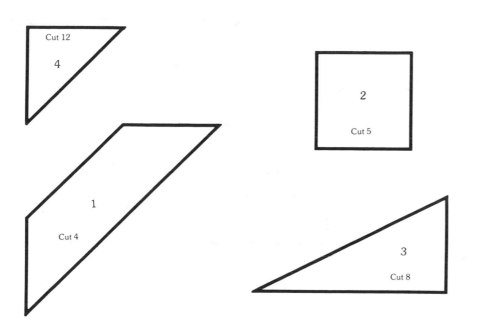

3
1
2

MEMORY
5" BLOCK

3
Cut 28

2
Cut 2

1
Cut 7

Cut 12
4

2
Cut 5

1
Cut 4

3
Cut 8

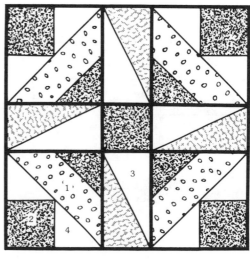

3
1
2
4

*HELEN'S STAR
5" BLOCK

Add Seam Allowance

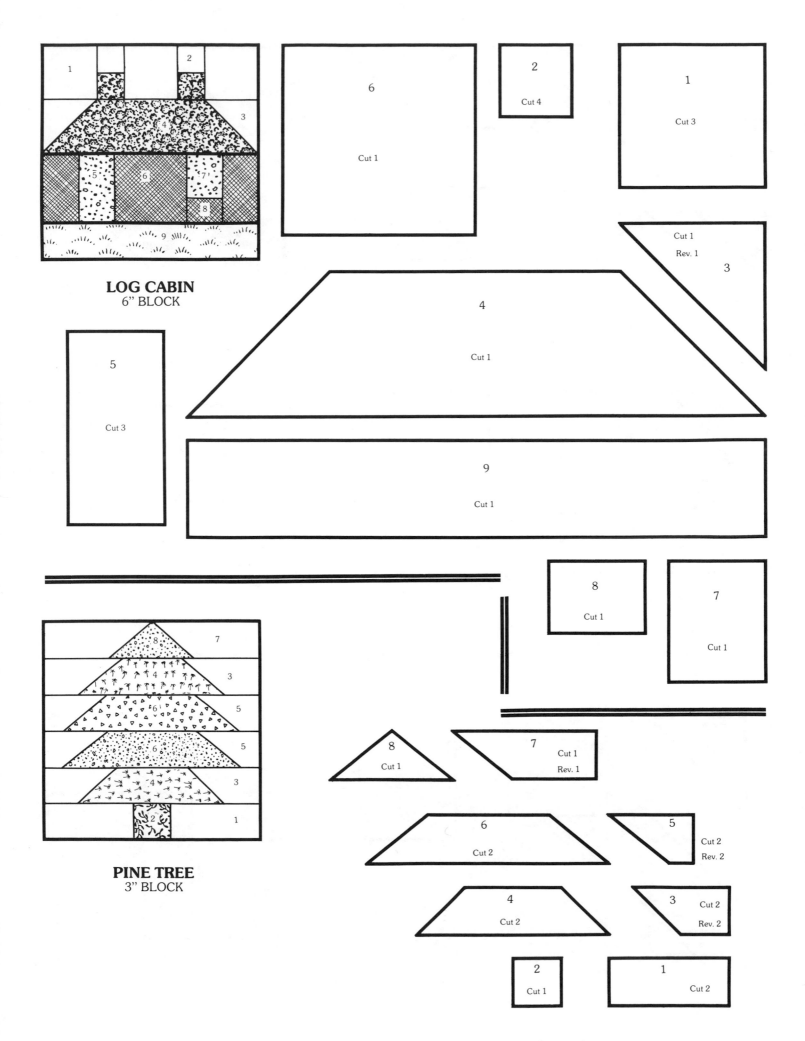

LOG CABIN
6" BLOCK

6
Cut 1

2
Cut 4

1
Cut 3

Cut 1
Rev. 1

3

4
Cut 1

5
Cut 3

9
Cut 1

8
Cut 1

7
Cut 1

PINE TREE
3" BLOCK

8
Cut 1

7
Cut 1
Rev. 1

6
Cut 2

5
Cut 2
Rev. 2

4
Cut 2

3
Cut 2
Rev. 2

2
Cut 1

1
Cut 2

Add Seam Allowance

72

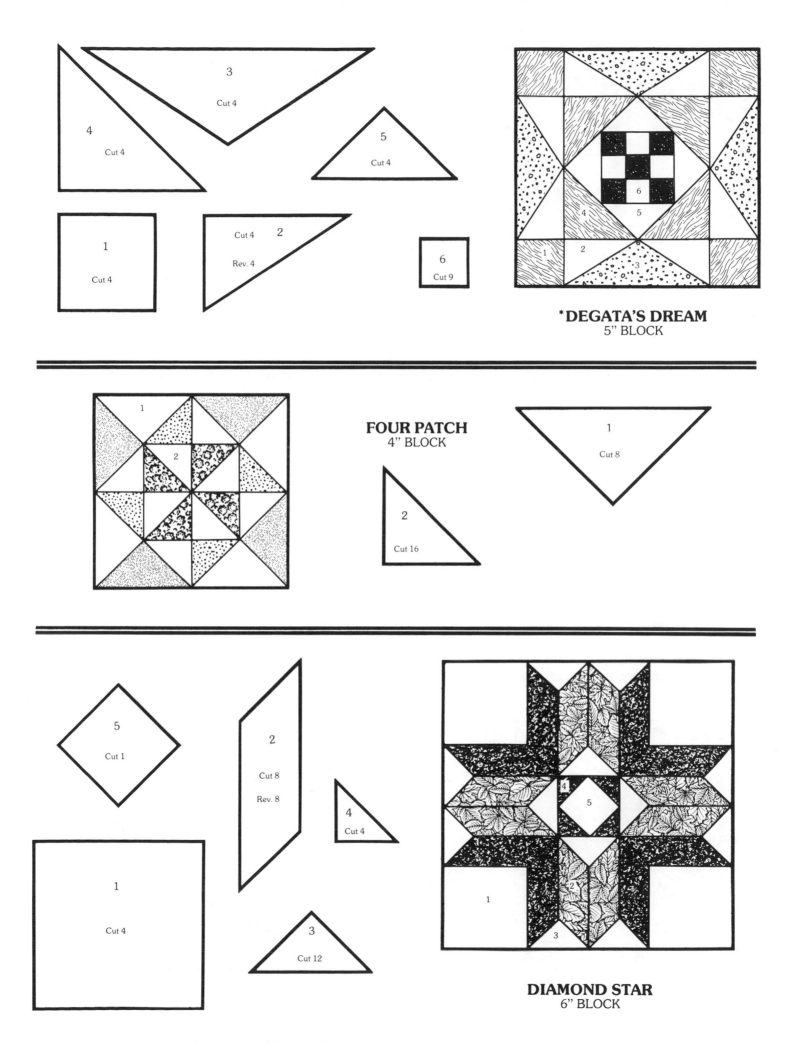

3
Cut 4

4
Cut 4

5
Cut 4

1
Cut 4

Cut 4
2
Rev. 4

6
Cut 9

*DEGATA'S DREAM
5" BLOCK

FOUR PATCH
4" BLOCK

1
Cut 8

2
Cut 16

5
Cut 1

2
Cut 8
Rev. 8

4
Cut 4

1
Cut 4

3
Cut 12

DIAMOND STAR
6" BLOCK

Add Seam Allowance

73

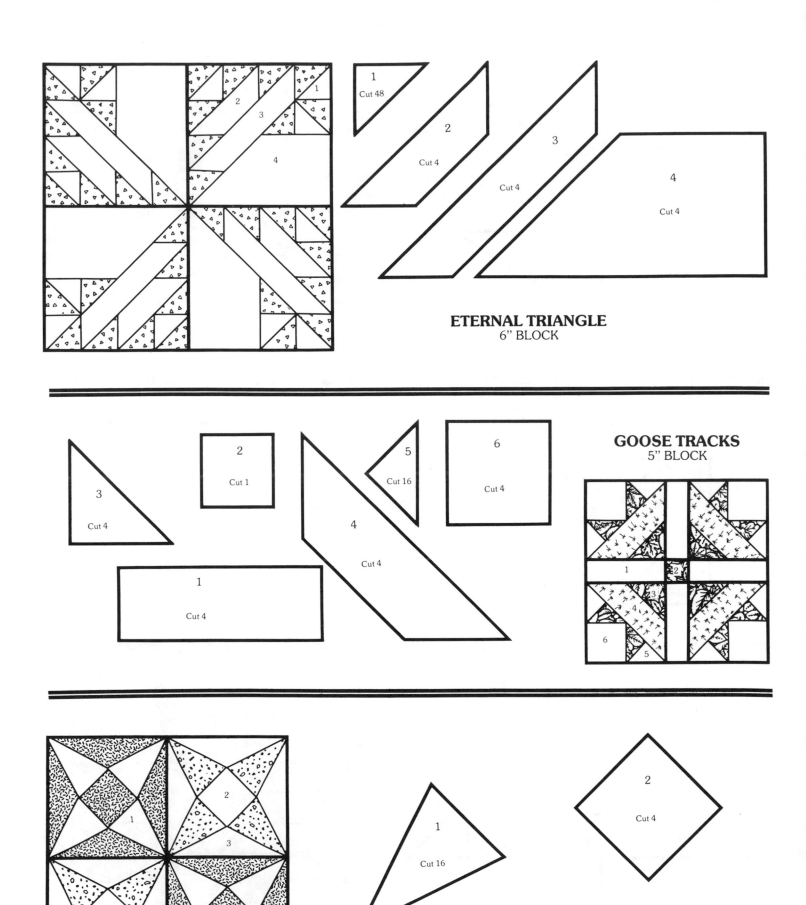

ETERNAL TRIANGLE
6" BLOCK

1
Cut 48

2
Cut 4

3
Cut 4

4
Cut 4

GOOSE TRACKS
5" BLOCK

3
Cut 4

2
Cut 1

5
Cut 16

6
Cut 4

4
Cut 4

1
Cut 4

WORLD WITHOUT END
6" BLOCK

1
Cut 16

2
Cut 4

3
Cut 16

Add Seam Allowance

74

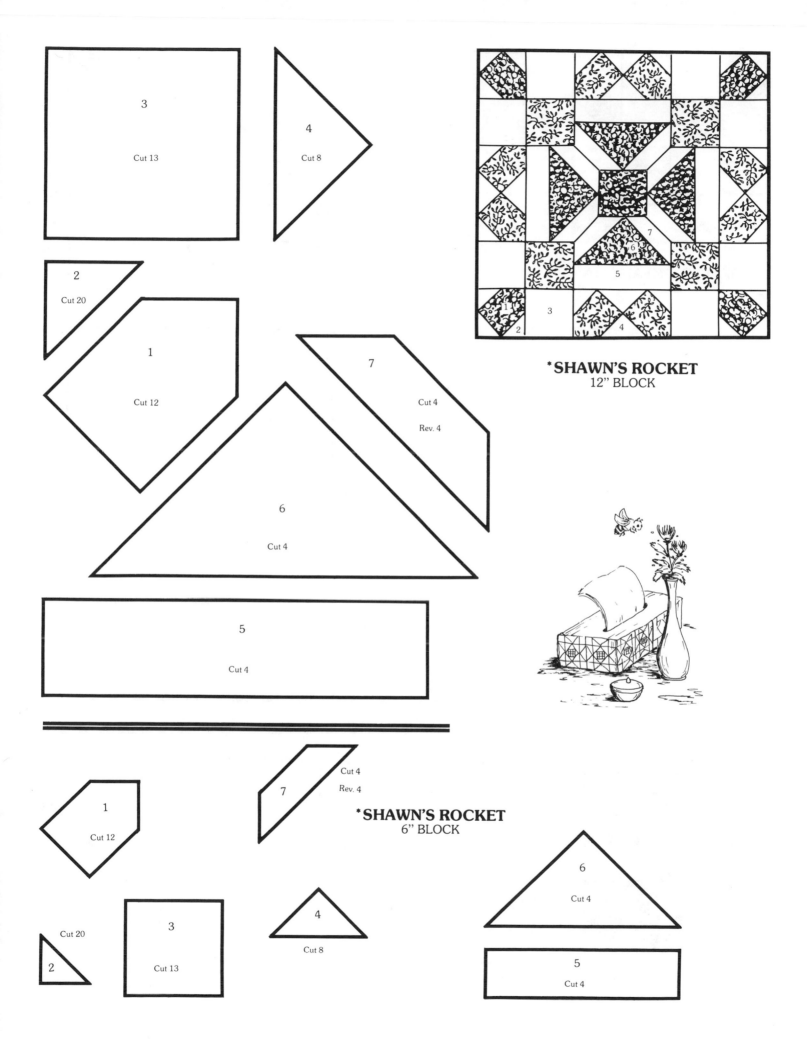

3

Cut 13

4

Cut 8

2

Cut 20

1

Cut 12

7

Cut 4

Rev. 4

6

Cut 4

5

Cut 4

*SHAWN'S ROCKET
12" BLOCK

7

Cut 4

Rev. 4

*SHAWN'S ROCKET
6" BLOCK

1

Cut 12

2

Cut 20

3

Cut 13

4

Cut 8

6

Cut 4

5

Cut 4

Add Seam Allowance

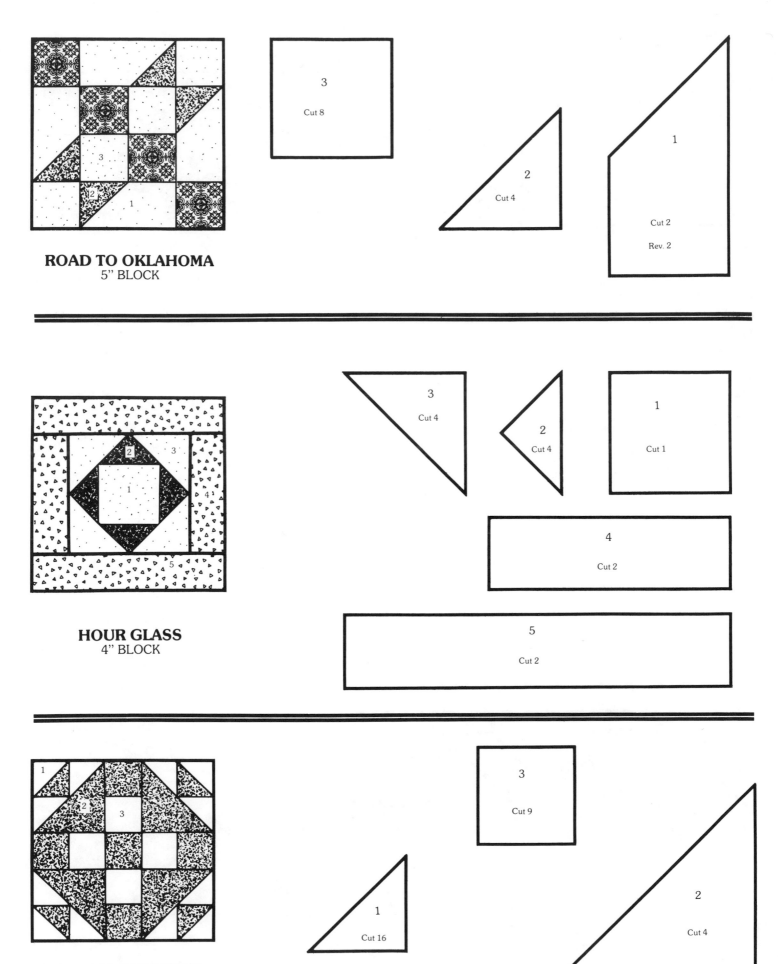

ROAD TO OKLAHOMA
5" BLOCK

3
Cut 8

2
Cut 4

1
Cut 2
Rev. 2

HOUR GLASS
4" BLOCK

3
Cut 4

2
Cut 4

1
Cut 1

4
Cut 2

5
Cut 2

HEN AND CHICKENS
5" BLOCK

3
Cut 9

1
Cut 16

2
Cut 4

Add Seam Allowance

HILL AND VALLEY
3" BLOCK

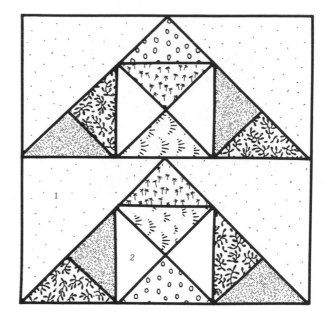

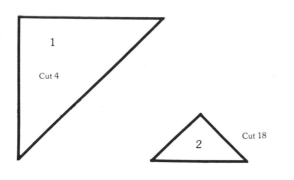

1

Cut 4

2

Cut 18

DOUBLE X
3" BLOCK

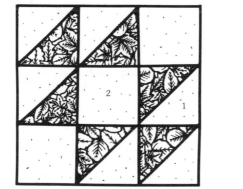

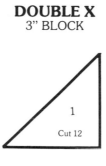

1

Cut 12

2

Cut 3

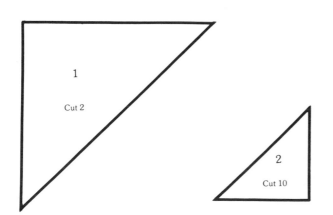

1

Cut 2

2

Cut 10

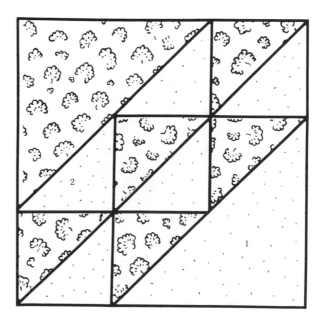

NORTH WIND
3" BLOCK

Add Seam Allowance

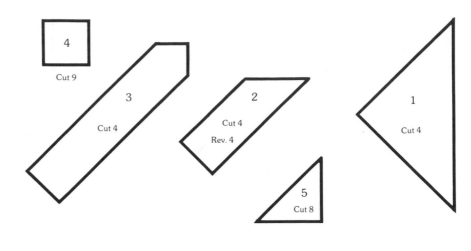

MEXICAN STAR
4" BLOCK

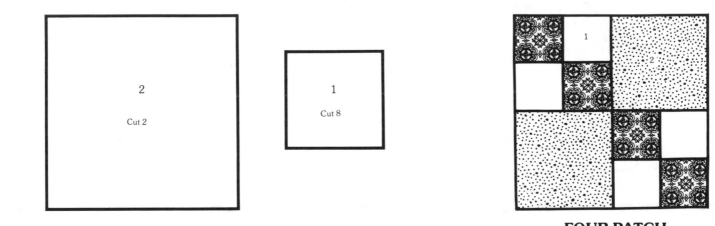

FOUR PATCH
4" BLOCK

KANSAS DUGOUT
4" BLOCK

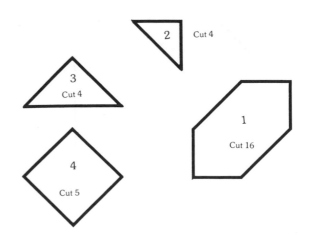

Add Seam Allowance

1

Cut 4

*HELEN'S CROWN
12" BLOCK

5

Cut 12

2

Cut 5

4

Cut 4

3

Cut 8

Rev. 8

6

Cut 4

Add Seam Allowance

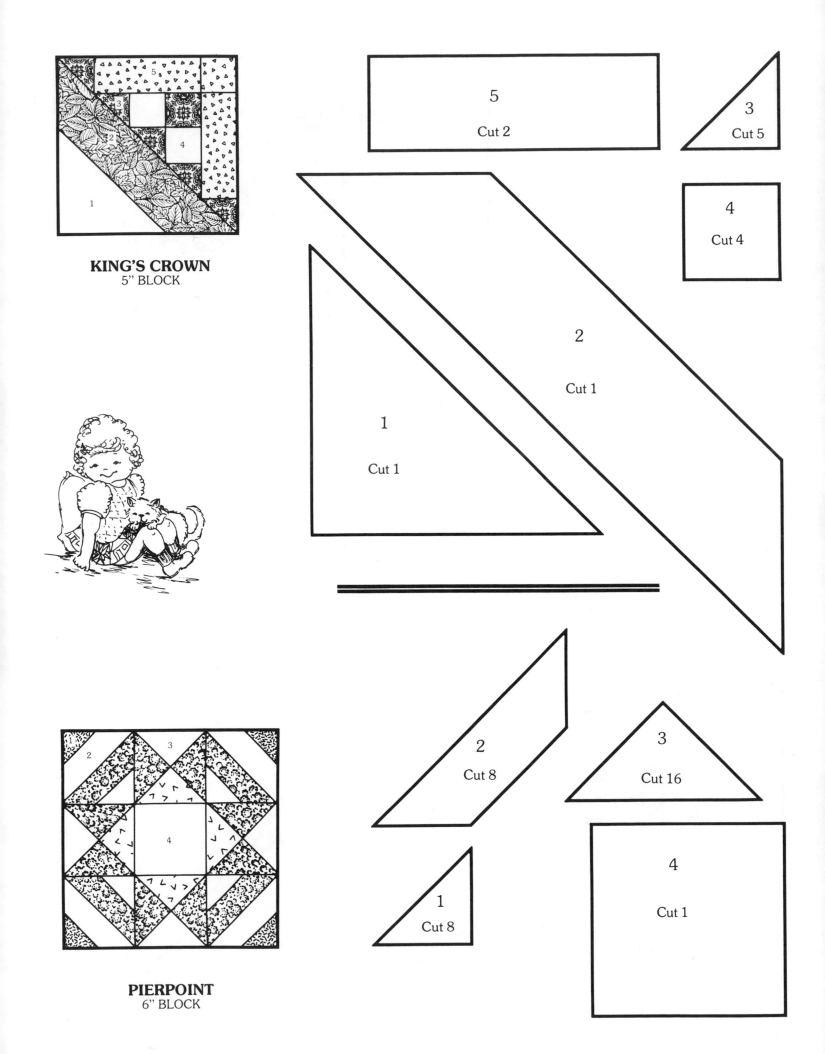

KING'S CROWN
5" BLOCK

5
Cut 2

3
Cut 5

4
Cut 4

2
Cut 1

1
Cut 1

PIERPOINT
6" BLOCK

2
Cut 8

3
Cut 16

1
Cut 8

4
Cut 1

Add Seam Allowance

2

Cut 8

1

Cut 20

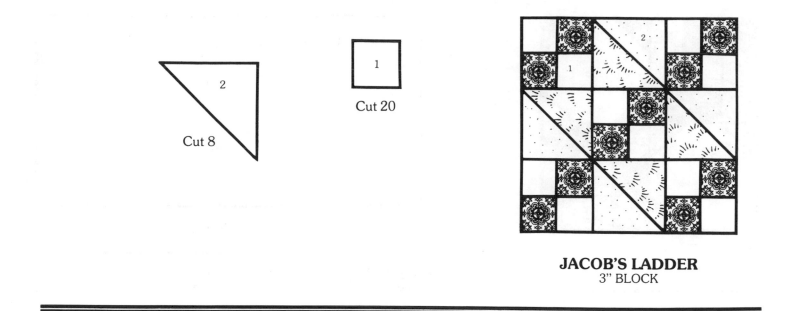

JACOB'S LADDER
3" BLOCK

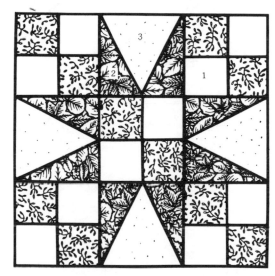

54-40 OR FIGHT
3" BLOCK

2

Cut 4

Rev. 4

3

Cut 4

1

Cut 20

1

Cut 5

2

Cut 16

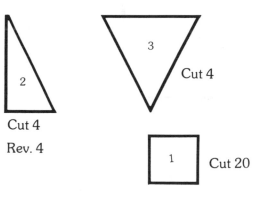

EIGHT POINT STAR
3" BLOCK

Add Seam Allowance

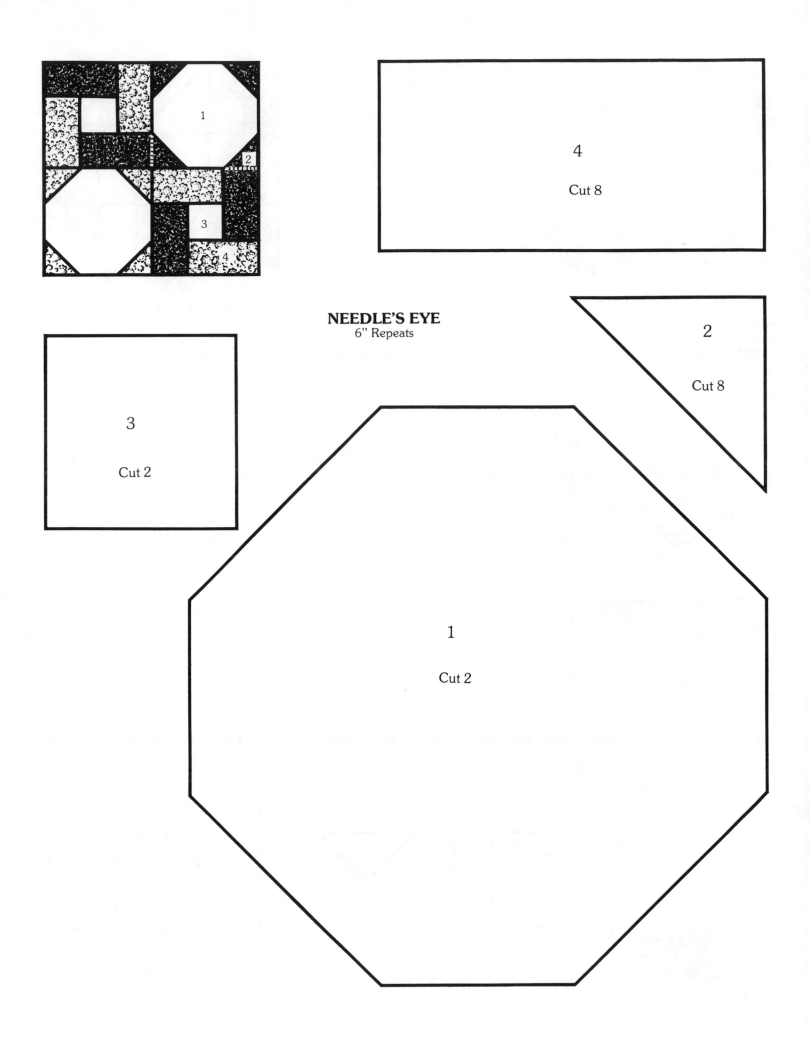

NEEDLE'S EYE
6" Repeats

4

Cut 8

3

Cut 2

2

Cut 8

1

Cut 2

Add Seam Allowance

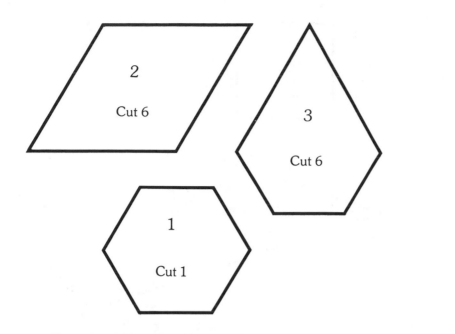

2

Cut 6

3

Cut 6

1

Cut 1

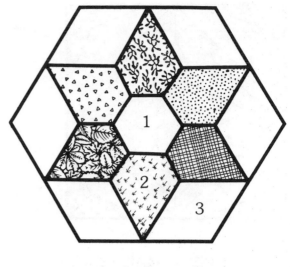

MISSOURI DAISY
5¼" Repeat

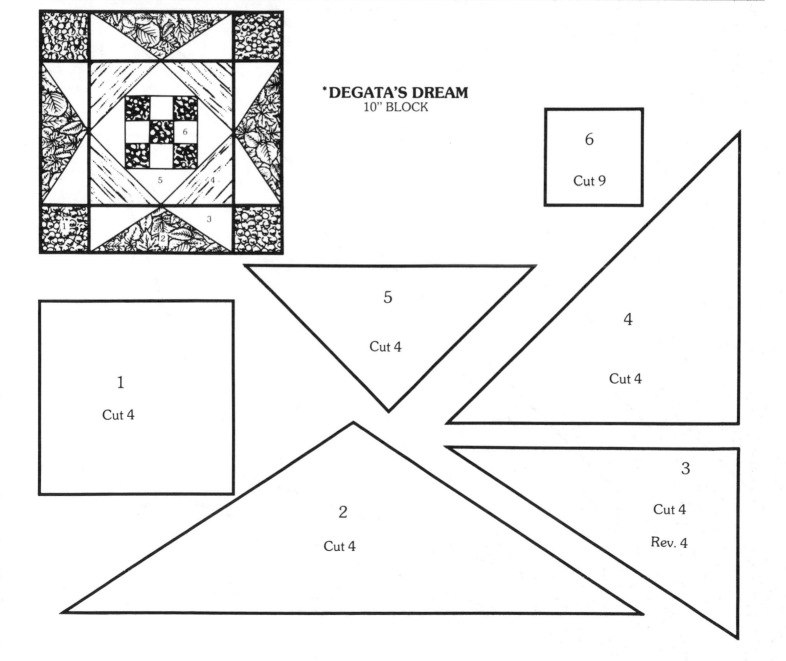

*DEGATA'S DREAM
10" BLOCK

6

Cut 9

5

Cut 4

4

Cut 4

1

Cut 4

3

Cut 4

Rev. 4

2

Cut 4

Add Seam Allowance

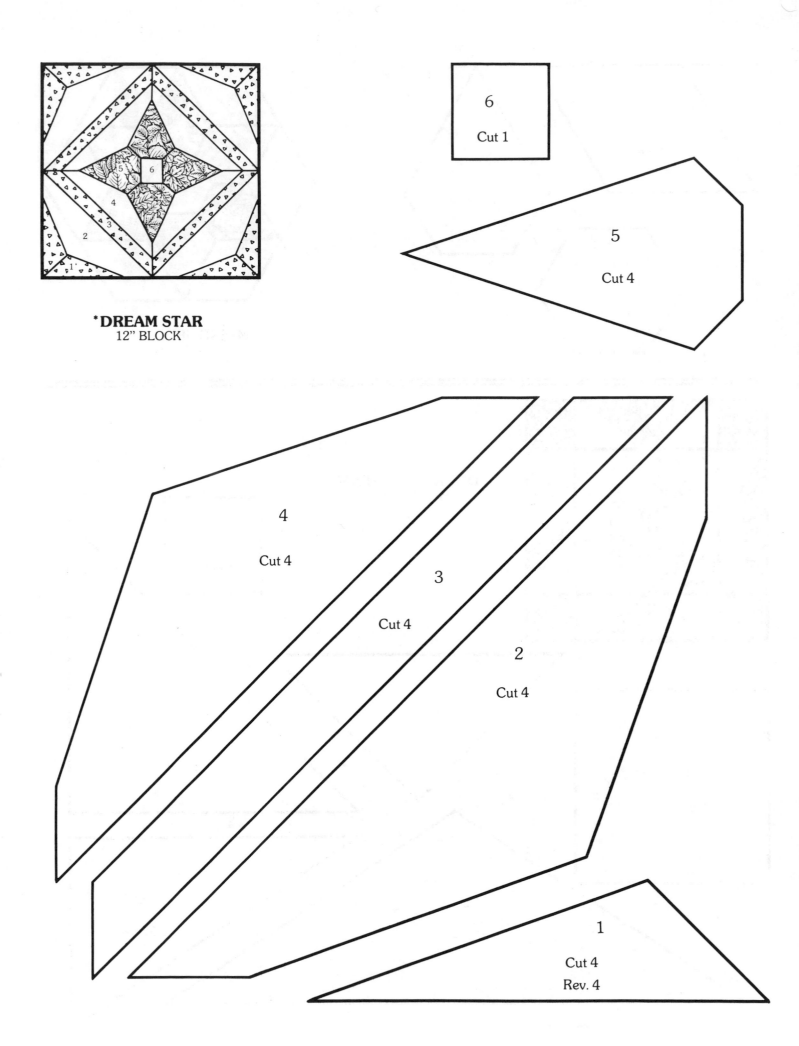

*DREAM STAR
12" BLOCK

6

Cut 1

5

Cut 4

4

Cut 4

3

Cut 4

2

Cut 4

1

Cut 4

Rev. 4

Add Seam Allowance

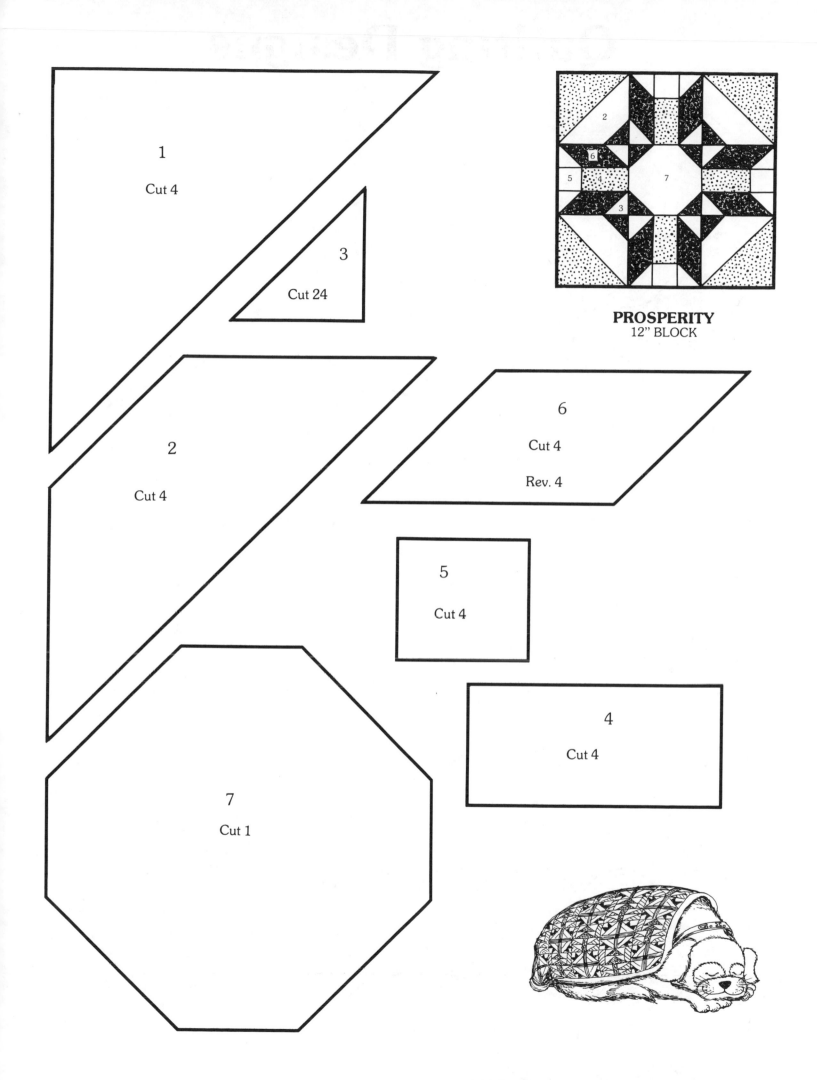

1

Cut 4

3

Cut 24

2

Cut 4

6

Cut 4

Rev. 4

5

Cut 4

4

Cut 4

7

Cut 1

PROSPERITY
12" BLOCK

Add Seam Allowance

Quilting Designs

Border Patterns

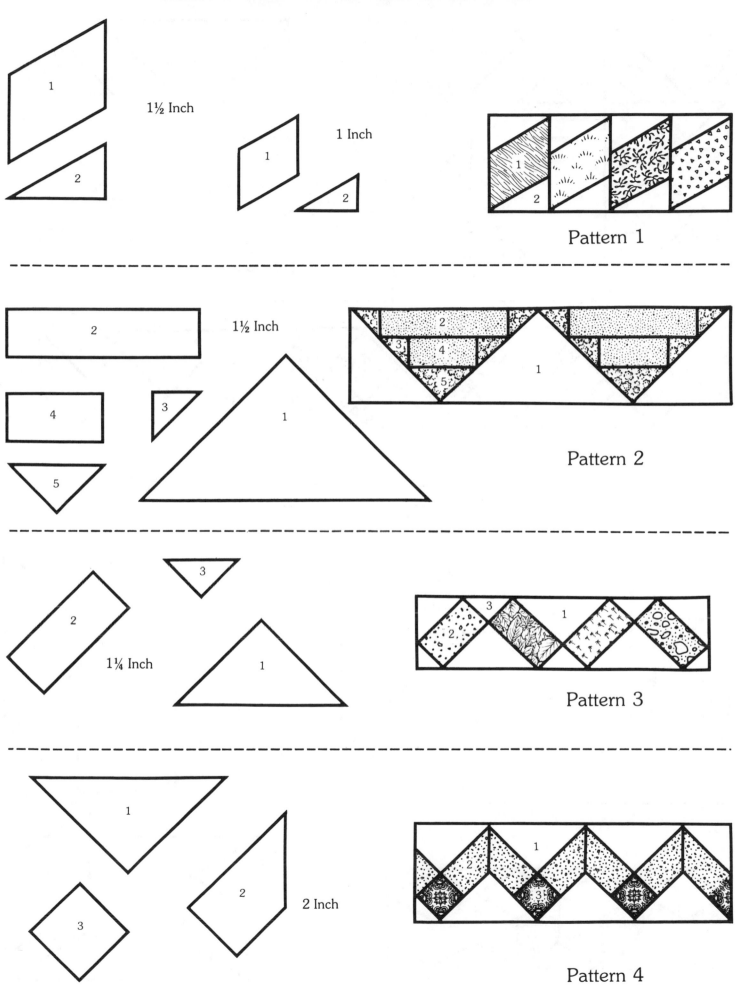

1½ Inch

1 Inch

Pattern 1

1½ Inch

Pattern 2

1¼ Inch

Pattern 3

2 Inch

Pattern 4

Add Seam Allowance

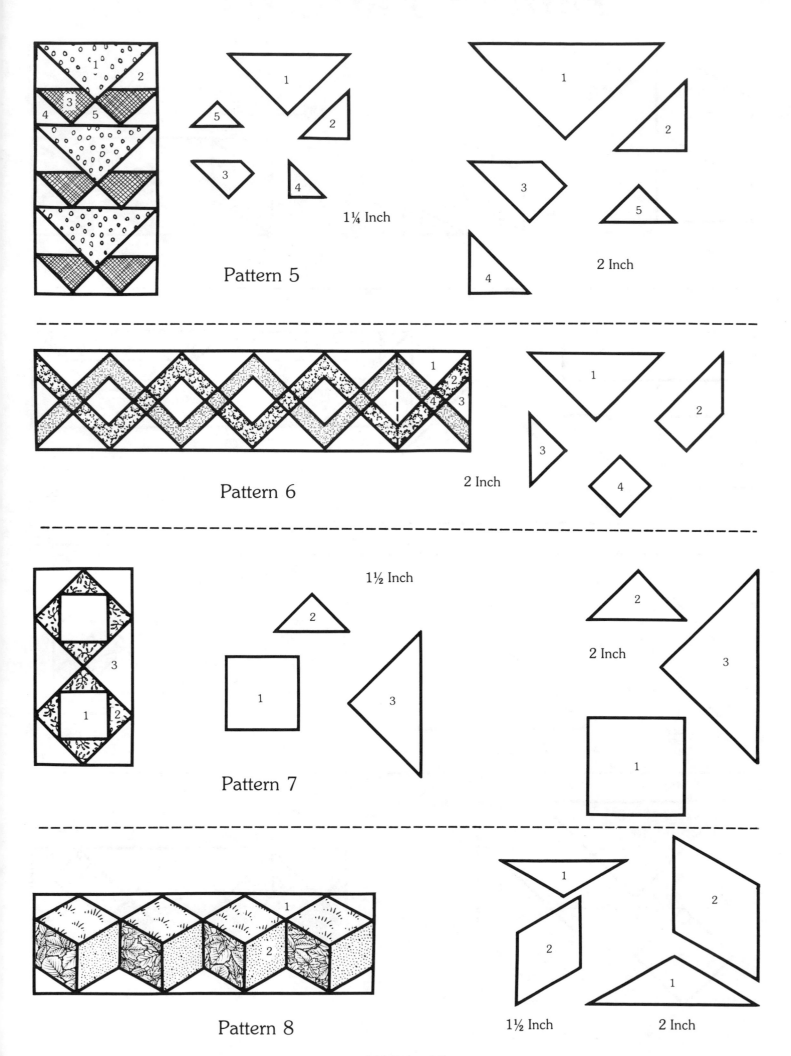

Pattern 5

5

1¼ Inch

2 Inch

Pattern 6

2 Inch

Pattern 7

1½ Inch

2 Inch

Pattern 8

1½ Inch   2 Inch

Add Seam Allowance

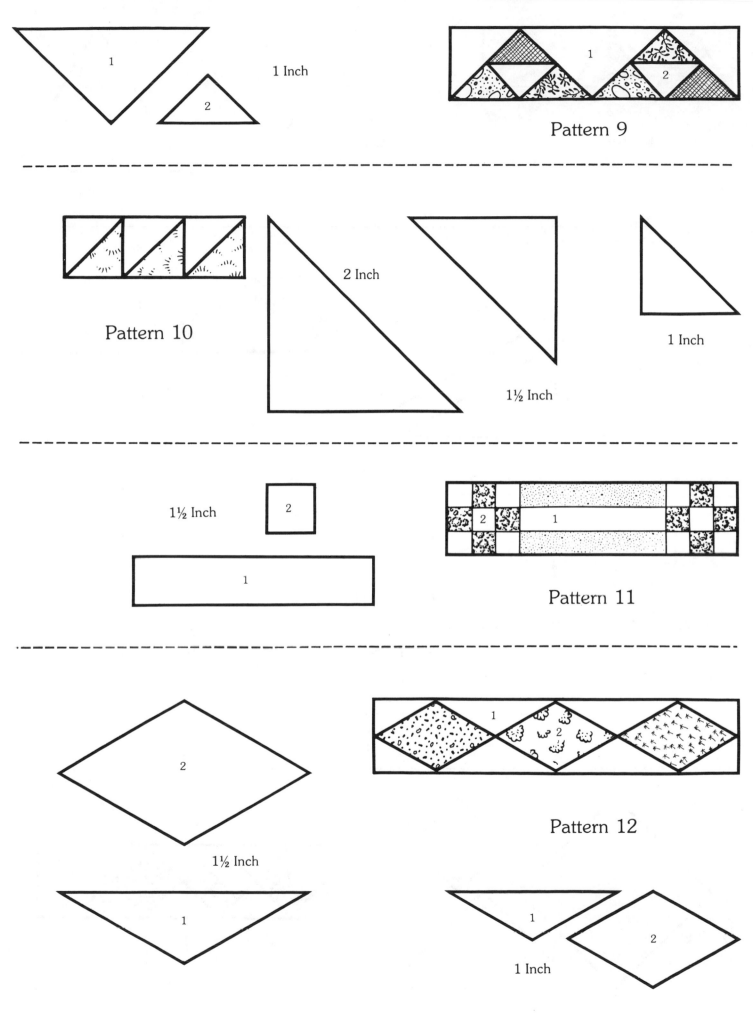

1 Inch

Pattern 9

Pattern 10

2 Inch

1½ Inch

1 Inch

1½ Inch

Pattern 11

Pattern 12

1½ Inch

1 Inch

Add Seam Allowance

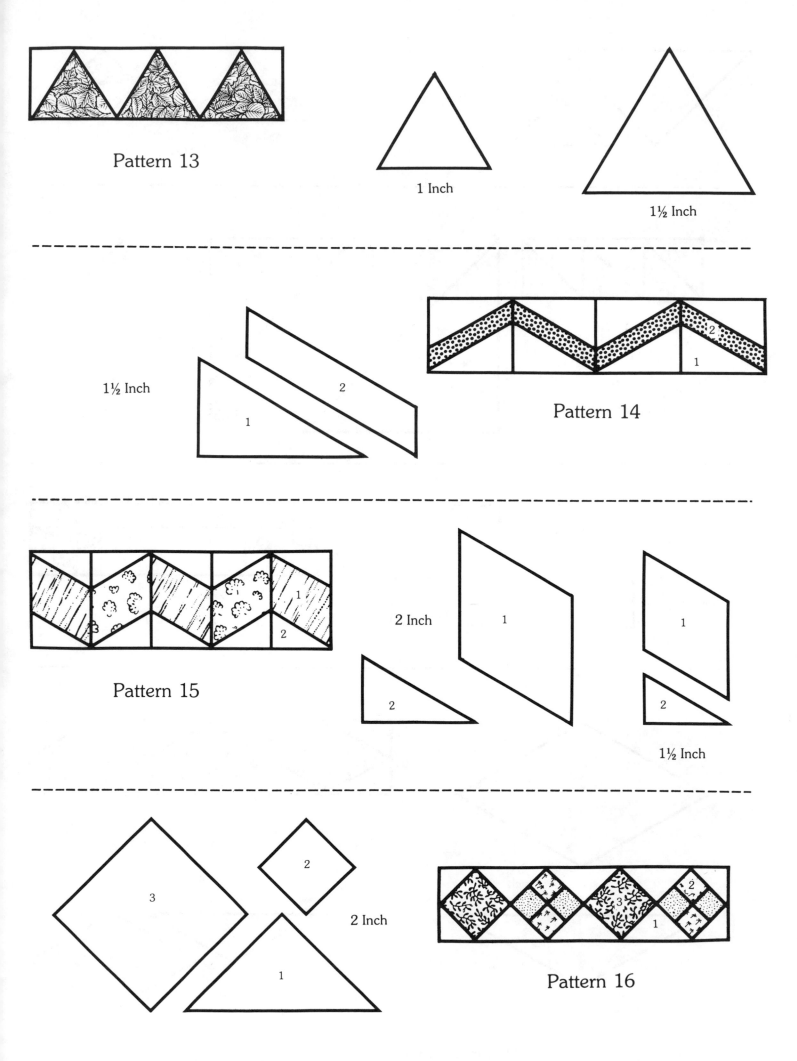

Pattern 13

1 Inch

1½ Inch

1½ Inch

Pattern 14

2

1

Pattern 15

2 Inch

1

2

1

2

1½ Inch

2

2 Inch

3

1

Pattern 16

Add Seam Allowance

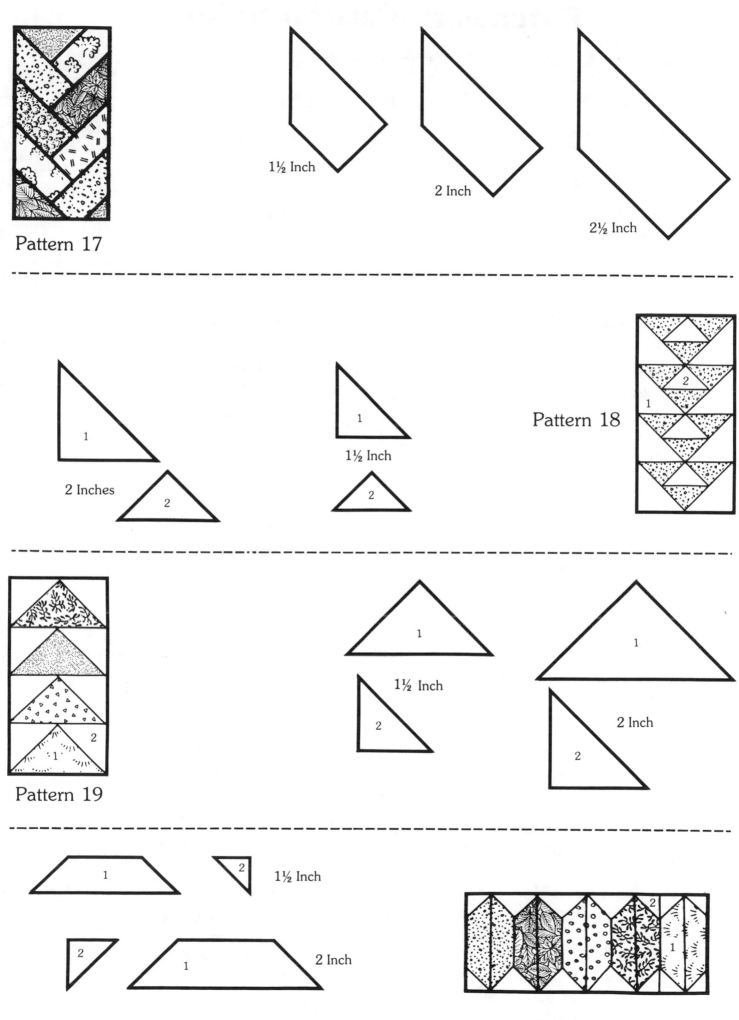

Pattern 17

1½ Inch

2 Inch

2½ Inch

1

2

2 Inches

1

2

1½ Inch

Pattern 18

Pattern 19

1

2

1½ Inch

1

2

2 Inch

1

2

1

2

1½ Inch

2

1

2 Inch

Add Seam Allowance

Pattern 20

Patchwork Pattern Index

*Original Designs

FULL-SIZED COMPANION BLOCKS

*Original Designs

BIBLIOGRAPHY

There are a great many excellent publications available today covering every phase of patchwork and quilting, from historical documentation to modern approaches to the craft; from beautiful color collections of museum quilts to current periodicals with up to the minute reportings of current happenings in the quiltmaking field. Within the following references may be found a rich sampling in each of the categories.

Bishop, Robert. *New Discoveries in American Quilts.*
    E.P. Dutton & Company. 1975

Finley, Ruth E. *Old Patchwork Quilts.*
    Charles T. Branford Co. 1971

Gutcheon, Beth. *The Perfect Patchwork Primer.*
    Penguin Books, 1974

Hall, Carrie A. and Rose G. Kretsinger. *The Romance of the Patchwork Quilt in America.*
    Caxton Printers LTD. 1935

Hinson, Delores A. *A Quilters Companion.*
    Arco Publishing, Inc. 1973

Holstein, Jonathan. *The Pieced Quilt.*
    New York Graphic Society, LTD. 1973

Ickis, Margaret. *The Standard Book of Quilt Making and Collecting.*
    Dover Publications, Inc. 1959

James, Michael. *The Quiltmaker's Handbook.*
    Prentice-Hall, 1978

Ladies Art Company Catalogue.
    Ladies Art Company, 1928

Orlafsky, Patsy and Myron. *Quilts in America.*
    McGraw-Hill Book Co., 1974

Peto, Florence. *Quilts and Coverlets.*
    Chanticleer Press. 1949

Puckett, Marjorie and Gail Giberson. *Primarily Patchwork.*
    Cabin Craft, 1975

Leman Publications, Inc., Wheatridge, Colorado. *Quilter's Newsletter Magazine.*
    (Periodical)